MEDIATION AND THE IMMEDIATE GOD

*Scriptures, the Church, and Knowing God*

# Mediation and the Immediate God

*Scriptures, the Church, and Knowing God*

Edith M. Humphrey

ST VLADIMIR'S SEMINARY PRESS

YONKERS, NY 10707

2023

**Publisher's Cataloging-in-Publication**
**(Provided by Cassidy Cataloguing Services, Inc.).**

Names: Humphrey, Edith M. (Edith McEwan), author.
Title: Mediation and the immediate God : scriptures, the Church, and knowing
God / Edith M. Humphrey.
Description: Yonkers, NY : St Vladimir's Seminary Press, [2023] | Includes
bibliographical references and index.
Identifiers: ISBN: 978-0-88141-744-9 (paperback) | 978-0-88141-745-6 (Kindle) |
LCCN: 2023933244
Subjects: LCSH: Mediation between God and man--Christianity. | Mediation-
-Religious aspects-- Orthodox Eastern Church. | God--Knowableness. | Jesus
Christ--Mediation. | Mary, Blessed Virgin, Saint--Mediation. | Saints--Mediation.
| Bible--Study and teaching. | Christian life. | Spiritual life--Orthodox Eastern
Church. | BISAC: RELIGION / Christianity / Orthodox. | RELIGION / Biblical
Studies / General. | RELIGION / Christian Living / Prayer.
Classification: LCC: BT640 .H86 2023 | DDC: 248.4/819--dc23

COPYRIGHT © 2023
ST VLADIMIR'S SEMINARY PRESS
575 Scarsdale Rd, Yonkers, NY 10707
1–800–204–2665
www.svspress.com

ISBN 978–0–88141–744–9 (paper)
ISBN 978–0–88141–745–6 (electronic)

The views of the authors of St Vladimir's Seminary Press books
do not necessarily reflect those of the Seminary.

PRINTED IN CANADA

*For my daughters Meredith, Alexandra, and Joëlle*
*who pour themselves out in motherly mediation on a regular basis!*

The publication of this book was made possible in part by a generous donation from Dr Don and Mrs Sue Tamulonis in honor of the Very Rev. Chad Hatfield for his many years of dedicated service to St Vladimir's Seminary and the Orthodox Church.

Other sponsors include Mr George Damous
and Ms Elizabeth Coelho.

# Table of Contents

# Preface

As I come to the end of this project—short in length, but lengthy in preparation—I am anticipating, with many brothers and sisters, the beginning of Great Lent. Towards the end of that preparation, we will mark the beginning of Holy Week, remembering the unrestrained appeal of the children in Jerusalem, "Hosanna! Lord, save us!" Their trusting cry is, perhaps, the most perfect picture of mediation that we can envisage. Jesus accepted their prayers on behalf of the people, and indeed said that if they did not cry out in this way, that the rest of creation—the very stones—would make up the deficit. It is a matter of human nature, it seems, to call out for help, not only for ourselves, but for others as well. In completing this study, I have a sense of only just beginning, for mediation is a many-faceted mystery whose depths can perhaps never be fully plumbed. I am thankful to many who have engaged me in this process: my long-suffering husband Chris; friends like Faye D'Ippolito, Nathan Graff, and Fr Tom Soroka; students who have heard me muse about this subject for several years; children who encountered me "playing" with it in my novel *Beyond the White Fence*; brothers and sisters from Holy Trinity Orthodox Cathedral (San Francisco) who heard my first formal thoughts on this during an Advent Retreat in 2019; generously broad-minded faculty and students from Canadian Mennonite University (Winnipeg), who heard drafted parts of the book when I gave the 2021 J. J. Thiessen lectures; and friends from

Houston Christian (Baptist) Seminary, who engaged me in lively conversation concerning these matters when I offered the 2022 A. O. Collins lecture. The receptivity and probing questions directed to me from young and mature, old friends and new acquaintances, academics and church members, Orthodox and others, have been invaluable. Most especially I am indebted to the incisive corrections and suggestions of my beloved editor, Fr Ignatius Green.

Every time I write, I am delighted to learn something that I did not know—something new (to me!) always emerges as fingers go to the keyboard, and then the work is further enriched by the hearing and response of others. Since this was a relatively new topic for one who has been Orthodox for about thirteen years, I made several discoveries, including the startling role of the angels, the significance of the whole creation, and the mediating presence seen in who we are, not simply what we do. I offer my investigation and meditations not in the first place to my Orthodox brothers and sisters (though I hope some will benefit), but especially to other Christian friends, hoping that they will be of interest to any who name Christ, or to those who want to listen in on a Christian household conversation. Since this is not an objective piece, but an in-house discussion, I frequently speak of "us," "we," and "our," and use Church Fathers alongside the Scriptures, parts of the liturgies, and contemporary authors in order to illustrate various points. It may be that sometimes the "our" does not ring true to every reader: if this is the case, forgive me for my presumption, and please take my inclusion as a mark of friendship! Where some of these resources may not be familiar to all readers, I have added footnotes to designate their origin and explain their significance. My prayer is that this little study will be of help in reframing the ongoing debate concerning mediation among those who love the Lord: in that sense, the book itself is intended as a form of "mediation" among friends.

Feast of the Meeting of the Lord in the Temple, 2023

# Introduction: Misgivings about Mediation?

"But this is the covenant which I will make with the house of Israel after those days," says the LORD: "I will put my law within them, and I will write it upon their hearts; and I will be their God, and they shall be my people. And no longer shall each man teach his neighbor and each his brother, saying, 'Know the LORD,' for they shall all know me, from the least of them to the greatest," says the LORD; "for I will forgive their iniquity, and I will remember their sin no more." Thus says the LORD, who gives the sun for light by day and the fixed order of the moon and the stars for light by night, who stirs up the sea so that its waves roar—the LORD of hosts is his name. (Jeremiah 31.33–35, RSV)

This luminous promise of the LORD,[1] reiterated in Hebrews 8.10–11, anticipates the New Covenant, longed for by God's

---

[1]Throughout this book, I will use the tradition adopted in those English translations of the Bible that render YHWH (Hebrew text) and KYRIOS (Greek text) by the word LORD in capitals, signifying the mystery of the name "I am." I will use this both for Old Testament and New Testament references, since to proclaim Jesus as LORD is to name Him not only in an honorific way, but as the One who spoke to Moses at the burning bush, the Holy God of all. As

ancient people and brought to us by the LORD Jesus. Unlike those who lived under the Old Covenant, where the operation of the Spirit's power was normally restricted to consecrated priests, inspired prophets, and anointed kings, Christians are not *foundationally* dependent upon other "special" Christians to have communion with God.

And so, long before the New Covenant was put in place, the great Moses rightly yearned *Would that all the LORD's people were prophets, that the LORD would put his Spirit upon them!* (Num 11.29, RSV). As the prophet Jeremiah affirms, those in the New Covenant depend personally upon God, for *they shall all know me, from the least of them to the greatest.* So it is that in 2 Corinthians 3–4 St Paul speaks about the removal of the "veil" from the eyes of God's people, that veil that hid from the general Hebrew community the *secret*—God embodied in Jesus—to which the Torah and Moses were pointing. Now, the apostle proclaims, we can "all," with unveiled faces, look upon and reflect the glory of the LORD (2 Cor 3.18). The creating God has brought about a new situation in which we all and each have seen *the light of the knowledge of the glory of God in the face of Jesus Christ* (2 Cor 4.6).[2]

If this is true, then why does "mediation" continue to be a natural part of our lives together in the Church? If the coming of the God-Man Jesus and the sending of the Holy Spirit to the Church have made God *im*mediate to us, so that each of us can speak directly with Him,[3] then why do we still pray for one another? Why do we still

---

Orthodox sing together at the beginning of the Matins service, "The LORD is God and has revealed himself to us" (Ps 117.27 LXX).

[2]Where Scripture passages are cited without a note regarding the translation, it is my own.

[3]I adopt the older tradition of using capitals for the masculine language of "He, Him, His" for God, and for any Person of the Trinity. This is to signal that masculine language for the Deity is both normative and mysterious—God is not male, but has revealed Himself in Scriptures and Tradition primarily

honor and defer to those who know Him well, and, in the apostolic Church, why do we pray with and to them? Why does the ancient Church revere, in icons, relics, songs, and petitions, those whom she calls "saints?" *Should* believers expect those faithful who have passed from this world to pray for them? Should they continue to pray for other loved ones who have passed into eternity? Is such mediation *passé*, a thing of the Old Covenant, or does it have a natural and continuing place among all of God's redeemed people—both those whom we still see, and those who are asleep in the LORD? And if mediation has a continuing important role, why is that so?

We know that these questions cause sharp disagreement among those who name Jesus, whom all Christians look to as our great Mediator. Indeed, such questions are intertwined with misunderstandings among Christians that seem nearly intractable. My hope is that this book will clarify some of the questions that we pose to each other on these matters, and help us to understand each other better, so that a real conversation can take place. I hope that it will also lift up the one perfect Mediator, the God-Man Jesus, while honoring those who are now in His direct presence, and see Him face to face.

My husband, who is a philosopher by discipline, reminds me that the matter of mediation and immediacy is also a philosophical problem. *Nothing* that we know is, strictly speaking, "immediate," for we know by means of data, interpreted through our bodies and minds. Furthermore, since the time of Kant, those who contemplate how humans are able to know things (the discipline of epistemology)

---

in masculine terms. For an argument concerning how this is a foundational matter for the Christian faith, see the final chapter in Edith M. Humphrey, *Further Up and Further In: Orthodox Conversations With C. S. Lewis on Scripture and Tradition* (Yonkers: St Vladimir's Seminary Press, 2017) and section IIC of Humphrey, *Ecstasy and Intimacy: When the Holy Spirit Meets the Human Spirit* (Grand Rapids, MI: Eerdmans, 2005).

have become more skeptical regarding our ability actually to know anything *in itself*: I can know my perception of a thing, such thinkers warn us, but I cannot know if I really know that thing! From the philosophical perspective, then, the title of this book may be ill-advised. If even the mundane things that we know require mediation, and we cannot be certain that we actually know these, then there surely can be no immediate experience of God, who is obviously far harder to understand than His creation.

But, of course, we use the word "immediate" in less absolute ways, don't we? Let's leave aside for the purposes of this discussion the Kantian problem of knowledge, which, if taken rigorously, would lead us to frozen inactivity and an absurd agnosticism of everything—including the paradoxical inability to know that we do not know. For those of us who are concerned about such matters, it may be helpful to adopt the perspective known as "critical realism."[4] This approach is "critical" because it acknowledges the problem of direct knowledge for embodied and limited persons. Yet it is "realistic" in that it also admits that if we are to talk about anything, human beings must assume that things around them do exist, and that we can have at least an approximate knowledge of them. From this commonsense perspective, I can speak of some of the knowledge that I have as *personally* immediate to me—that is, I know the thing or I know the person because of my own connection to the object that is perceived, and not simply on the authority of someone else. This kind of knowledge is true in general living, and also, it appears, in the spiritual realm.

---

[4]This approach is frequently associated in the secular world with Roy Bhaskar and Michael Polanyi, but it has been variously adapted and helpfully employed by theologians and biblical scholars such as T. F. Torrance, Alister McGrath, Ben F. Meyer, James Dunn, and N. T. Wright.

Consider the case of the Samaritans, who were witnessed to by the woman who met Jesus at the well (traditionally named Photini, the "illumined one," among Orthodox Christians). Yes, they heard about Jesus the Messiah by means of her words. But then they invited Him to stay with them, and heard His teaching for two days (Jn 4.40). After this, *They said to the woman, "It is no longer because of what you have said that we believe, for we have heard him ourselves, and we know that this is truly the Savior of the world"* (Jn 4.42, RSV). His dwelling with them transformed a mediated word into an immediate encounter, and so they believed *for themselves*: there were now several hundred Samaritan "Photinis," or illumined ones, and not simply one.

This was possible because the almighty LORD has the wherewithal and the desire to take upon Himself (as the Church Fathers put it, to "assume") everything that it is to be human and to *dwell* with and among us. And He has done so! What happened to the Samaritan community is also true of us personally. As St Paul declares, *The word is near you, on your lips and in your heart* (Rom 10.8, RSV). As the risen Jesus promises in the book of Revelation, *Behold, I stand at the door and knock; if any one hears my voice and opens the door, I will come in to him and eat with him, and he with me* (Rev 3.20, RSV). God engages, then, to work personally with us, face to face and heart to heart, and He does this both as the Second Person of the Holy Trinity (the Son) names each of us His brother or sister (Heb 2.11), and as the Third Person of the Trinity (the Holy Spirit) comes to dwell within each of us.

Yet the corporate nature of Christ's Body, the Church, is also an integral part of the good news. We frequently miss this emphasis when we read contemporary English translations of the Bible, which cannot easily distinguish, in the absence of the archaic "thee, thou, thine," between the singular "you" and the plural "you." As a result,

many of the assurances and the promises given by God to His people
as a whole are mistakenly assumed by the contemporary reader primarily to address the individual. There are, rather, far more passages
in the Scriptures that speak about God's presence with His Body,
among us, than with individuals! Orthodox believers are reminded of
this almost weekly with the salutation and response: "Christ is *among
us!*"; "He is and ever shall be!"

Moreover, even those passages that suggest an individual relationship with God involve other believers. Consider again the two
passages concerning the Samaritans and the knocking Jesus. The
Samaritans came to have a personal connection with the LORD, but
it was at first mediated to them by Photini. Jesus promises the luke-
warm Laodiceans that each of them may have a deep and passionate
relationship with Him—if he or she opens the door. But this promise
is transmitted to us today by means of several layers of mediation:
Jesus, with the approval of the Father, has appeared in a vision to John
(Rev 1.1); He has addressed Himself to the "angel" of each church
(e.g., Rev 2.1); the contents of His messages to the seven churches
have been written down at Christ's command (Rev 1.19); they have
been gathered together with other visions in the Apocalypse (Rev
22.8–9); that book has finally been read and validated as Holy Scripture by diverse communities of the holy Church, West and East; and
we read it in our own languages by means of translators. As the first
verse of the Apocalypse (which is actually a lengthy title) puts it,
this is *The revelation of Jesus Christ, which God gave him to show to his
servants . . . and he made it known by sending his angel to his servant
John* (Rev 1.1, RSV). The process has involved Jesus, angels, visions,
words, John the visionary, scrolls and codices, and the work of our
older siblings in the faith. It seems, then, that mediation is the norm
even when we are given examples or teaching concerning immediacy
with God.

In all this we may perceive a tension or a paradox surrounding the question of how we know *about* God and also how we come to *know* Him: God can and does come to each of us personally; yet God normatively has used and continues even under the New Covenant to use others in order to reveal Himself to us. Of course, mediation is a large category, not restricted only to prayer, and it also includes actions of teaching, reconciling, healing, and interpreting: literally, it means to "go between" one person and another. Mediation, then, refers to any action in which a person stands between two others, as a bridge. In our Christian Tradition it evokes the action of a faithful and compassionate person (or being) who stands between someone or something else in creation and God, linking them together in some way. In Galatians 3.19, for example, St Paul speaks about the Law given both through the angels and a (human) mediator (i.e., Moses), and contrasts this first situation with the New Covenant, which comes through Jesus alone. In this book, we will concentrate mostly upon the aspect of prayer one for another, or intercession, while acknowledging the broader aspects of mediation.

We should remember, too, that prayer is a broad concept in itself, since it includes various other acts besides that of intercession. There are, of course, numerous excellent books and guides to prayer in general, written both in antiquity and more recently; this study does not seek to add to them. Instead, I hope to consider that particular component of prayer in which we petition God on behalf of others, or in which others speak to God for us, and place these "mediating" actions ("intercession") alongside other modes of mediation within the Christian family. How intercession and petition fit together with adoration, confession, and thanksgiving will emerge at certain places in our discussion; however, my aim is not to give any kind of taxonomy or guide to prayer in general, but to keep the focus quite narrow.

A study of mediation in itself, we will see, is deep and broad enough to occupy us for some time!

I invite you, then, to explore this mystery of mediating prayer with me, by looking to the Scriptures, as interpreted by those who have come before us, some of whom Christians have honored with the title "Church Fathers." We will start by establishing the profound significance of mediation for our faith, beginning, as is fitting, with the "one Mediator" between God and man, the God-Man, our LORD Jesus. Our departure point for this first chapter will be 1 Timothy 2 (where the title of mediator is given to Jesus), followed by the Letter to the Hebrews (a sermon that highlights His mediation), and ending with the Fourth Gospel (which presents the Logos by whom all knowledge of the Father is mediated). We will then go on in the second chapter of the study to consider the matter of our mediation for each other, which is also discussed in 1 Timothy 2. Here, we will ask why, in light of what we know about the Church, this activity remains important. Key to this second chapter will be Jesus' description of prayer in the Gospels, portions of Paul's letters in which he describes our interconnections, and the early history concerning human mediation transmitted through the Acts of the Apostles. Next, Chapter Three will consider mediation across the "divide" of death—seen both in the prayers of the living for the "dead," and in the prayers of the saints for others. Attention will then be given to the strange role of angels in our salvation, as well as to the role of physical objects (the eucharistic elements, relics, and icons) in our petitions and intercessions. We will finish this third chapter by delving into what Scripture teaches and does not teach concerning those who have departed from our midst, and address the concerns that some contemporary Christians have regarding necromancy (the magical use of the dead) and presumption. This means to note carefully the difference between authentic Christian petition (which assumes that God is the ultimate Giver of all good things) and ancient ideas of magic, or contemporary notions of "positive thinking." Chapter Four examines what seems to be a special "charism" of mediation among female figures (especially in Matthew's Gospel), and looks to the particular role of the Virgin Mary, historically considered the mediatrix *par excellence* both in the West and in the East. In our conclusion we will contemplate both how our understanding of the Church and our intercommunion with each other are forged by our dependence upon each other, as expressed in petitionary and intercessory prayer. In the final analysis, mediation will be seen to be an essential mark of the Church that God uses for our full salvation.[5]

[5]"Salvation," which comes from a root word having to do with "health," is understood in various ways among Christians. For some, it has a narrow meaning, and refers only to the specific work of Christ, especially what He wrought upon the cross for us. However, it is clear from St Paul's use of it in 1 Corinthians 7.16, where the "wife" is pictured as a means of salvation for her husband, that the word can be used more broadly, referring to all that goes into our maturity as sons and daughters of God. In this study, I will use the broader sense of "salvation," while restricting "redemption" to refer to the unique work of the God-Man, Jesus, and how He rescued us from sin and death. Of course, anything used for our healing and well-being—whether physical, mental, or spiritual—ultimately comes from God Himself, but we will see how some of the facets of salvation come to us through God's creation and creatures.

# CHAPTER I

# There is One God and One Mediator

I remember how as an older child and teen who was nurtured in the Canadian Salvation Army, I sang with gusto a "chorus" that (I think) is particular to the Army:

> For there is one God and one mediator, 'twixt God
>     and man
> For there is one God and one mediator—the Man
>     Christ Jesus,
> Who gave Himself a ransom for us all, Who gave
>     Himself a ransom for us all,
> Who gave Himself a ransom for us all—Oh, what a
>     wonderful Saviour!
> For there is one God and one Mediator 'twixt God
>     and man,
> For there is one God and one Mediator—the Man
>     Christ Jesus!

This chorus, of course, is a versification of the text in 1 Timothy 2.5–6, and its focus is, as it should be, on the glory of the God-Man, our Savior. But I am fairly sure that, as we sang it, some of the more informed Salvationists understood it also to be a cry of protest against other forms of Christianity that looked to saints for mediating help.

Only this connection accounts for the militant rhythm in which the chorus was sung, and the atmosphere that it evoked, akin to a team pep rally. *We* took the Scriptures seriously, and did not let any superstition or ossifying accretions weigh down our understanding of the uniqueness of Christ. As with the Army's rejection of Baptism, *nothing* was necessary for the Christian except bare-naked faith. Indeed, these verses from 1 Timothy are understood not only by my childhood community, but by numerous other Protestant assemblies as a straightforward scriptural rejection of any mediators besides the LORD Jesus Himself. For this reason, before we can go on to explore the positive teaching concerning Jesus and mediation in Hebrews and the Fourth Gospel, we must carefully address this statement concerning Jesus as the *only* mediator.

*The Great Mediation*

Certainly these verses in 1 Timothy pose a challenge for those who would tackle the subject of mediation, in the same way as the words of Jesus so often quoted by Protestants: "Call no man 'father.'" After my earliest formation in the Salvation Army, when I was an Anglican for a quarter of a century, I learned to detect the ecclesial beliefs of clergy whom I met in this diverse community by whether or not they accepted the title Father (or Mother) So-and-So. The refusal of that honorific was inevitably accompanied by a less mystical view of the sacraments, an understanding of ordination as pragmatic rather than charismatic, a view of the threefold office (episcopate-presbyterate-diaconate) as non-essential, and a downplaying of the role of saints and the Theotokos (the "God-Bearer" Mary) in the life of the Church. For me, the question was raised: is this "low-church" view of these interrelated matters in the Church a Protestant novelty, or is it a correct reading of the pertinent passages in Scripture?

As a first principle, most agree that we ought not pick and choose among passages in Scripture in order to bolster our own theology. Rather, the whole of Scripture must inform our views, our structures, and our actions. Concerning both Jesus' words regarding "father" and the declaration concerning "one Mediator," we encounter a puzzle when we go to the Bible as a whole: if taken as absolutes, these two statements are contradicted elsewhere in holy writ. It would seem that St Paul was ignorant of Jesus' prohibition, since he calls himself "father" to the Corinthians, and urges them to accept his authority as such (1 Cor 4.15). Further, in both Galatians 1.14 and Hebrews 1.1, as well as throughout the Gospels (e.g., Lk 1.55, 72; 16.24; Jn 6.49; 7.22), the noteworthy figures of the past are referred to as "our fathers." One might counter that, for the most part, these are references to actual physical ancestors, rather than spiritual honorifics: obviously Jesus' words are not intended to dissuade children from respecting their actual fathers, or ancestors, as in the habit adopted by some contemporary families starting in the 1970s, where Mom's and Dad's first name is impertinently on the child's lips. But it would seem that the New Testament does *not* restrict the meaning of "father" in this way: there are several places where "father" is used not of physical, but of spiritual ancestors in the faith. The most obvious here would be Paul's application of "father" to Abraham regarding the Gentiles, who have no physical connection with that patriarch.

If, in fact, Jesus intended His community not to use the title "father" in a metaphorical, spiritual, or ecclesial sense, His followers seem not to have gotten the memo. Besides the case of Abraham, we find the title used with respect by the deacon Stephen (Acts 7.2), by the apostle Paul in addressing the Jewish leaders (Acts 22.1), and also in the Letter of John to address Christian leaders (1 John 2.13–14). It would seem, then, that Jesus' words were not taken literally by His followers, who continued to refer to their biological *and* spiritual leaders in this familial way. Instead, His teaching "call no man father" may be taken as a way of establishing the utter *uniqueness* of God as Father, a perspective more fully explained by the apostle in Ephesians: *For this reason I bow my knees before the Father, from whom all fatherhood* [or every family under a father] *in heaven and on earth is named* (Eph 3.14–15). To recognize God as *the* Father, the only source of all things, is a much more powerful stance than simply to formally refrain from referring to others in this way! Christianity, it would seem, has both an iconoclastic *and* an iconic impulse, which at first blush would seem to contradict each other: God is the only absolute Father; yet, because of His image imprinted on His creatures, we rightly see a reflected radiance and call others "father," to His glory.

A similar situation is to be found with regard to the idea of mediation. Throughout this book we will explore how our brothers and sisters, our fathers and mothers in Christ, are meant to mediate, that is, to bring us to understand God better: this is what it means to be in the Christian family. But it is good and right for us to begin with the One, the unique Mediator, the God-Man, Jesus our Savior. These verses in 1 Timothy should be understood for their positive and transformational significance, not simply as a shibboleth or rally cry against Christians who revere the saints of the past. So, what did the apostle mean when he spoke of Jesus as the *one* Mediator?

It is useful to read the verses in context, with the help of some ancient theologians of the Church. The first thing to notice is that the main topic of this passage is mediation in general, as practiced by the Christian community: *First of all, then, I urge that entreaties, prayers, intercessions, and thanksgivings be made for all people. . .* (1 Tim 2.1). So then, Jesus' status as the *only* mediator comes to us within a passage that envisages us all as mediators, when we intercede with God on behalf of others. Why not let folks simply pray for themselves, for the God-Man is the only Mediator who truly loves them and has the power to act for their well-being? Yet we are called, because we are Christians, to pray—a form of standing between God and the one for whom we are praying. Still the question remains: if mediation is truly the task of God's Body, why does the apostle go on to characterize Jesus as unique in this respect?

We notice in the flow of the letter's argument that the call to intercede on behalf of all, including non-Christian leaders, is explained both in pragmatic terms (it will afford peace to the community, 2.2) and in theological terms (God loves all and wills their salvation, 2.3–4). As we reflect on God's will in this matter, however, we become aware of a problem: it is not certain that all *shall* be saved, despite God's *will*. So, then, the passage goes on immediately to speak about the grounds of our redemption—Jesus, the *one* Mediator between God and humanity (2.5), who gave Himself as a "ransom" (2.6). The passage thus joins together God's will with God's action—the *one* true God wills for all to be saved, and so the *one* Mediator became our ransom. Oneness, of course, is the most basic characteristic of the true God, as the Hebrew people reminded themselves daily with the Shema of Deuteronomy 6.4: *Hear, O Israel, the* LORD *our God is one*. Christians cleave to the same teaching, as Paul reminds us in 1 Corinthians 8.4: *an idol has no real existence and . . . there is no God but one*, now known in the Father, Son, and Holy Spirit.[1]

---

[1] 1 Corinthians 8 actually only introduces the reader to the first two Persons of the Holy Trinity, as St Paul reformulates the Shema for the Christian community, associating the Father with the name "God," and the Son with the name "LORD" (YHWH, "the Existing One.") But in his second letter to the Corinthians, St Paul supplements this "binitarian" view by speaking of the Holy Spirit as "the LORD" (2 Cor 3.18), and so we see an early attempt to articulate the mystery of the Trinity here, as elsewhere in his letters.

In this vein, the blessed Augustine reads 1 Timothy's words regarding Jesus as the *one* Mediator as a *caveat* for those who wrongly suppose that the accomplishment of God's will might come through good human living alone, without partaking of the Body and Blood of Christ.[2] We may expand on St Augustine's thought as we read 1 Timothy 2. Here we learn that Jesus is the mediator of our redemption; further, prayers are to be offered in His name for others, no matter what their position in society, in hope that they will respond to God's love. It is because of Jesus' ransom that St Paul enjoins our prayers for others in verses 1–3, but prayers are not magic. Cooperation with God is indicated at every level—when we intercede for others, and when they respond to God—while the initiative for our redemption is from God alone. To the first half of the verse in question (*there is one God and one mediator between God and humans*) we must add the second: *the (hu)man Christ Jesus, who gave himself a ransom for us all.* The verse thus interprets itself for us, showing the specific way in which Jesus is the unique Mediator. He alone is the ransom.

This leads us to make another observation: the Mediator of our redemption is a human among humans, "the (*Hu*)*Man*[3] Christ Jesus."

[2] *Letter* 149.2.17; *St Augustine, Letters*, Volume 3 (131–164), trans. Sr Wilfrid Parsons, S.N.D., Fathers of the Church 20 (Washington, DC: Catholic University of America Press, 1947), 252.

[3] An earlier age that could use "Man" without discomfort had beneficial access to a word that could mean both an individual human being, and humanity in general: "This man called John"; "Man is a thinking animal." Unfortunately, the emphasis upon exclusionary language has deprived our day of such a word, even while the contemporary use of the word "human being" and "humanity" (rather than "Man") helpfully reminds us of the significance of women as well as men. Greek and Hebrew may more easily distinguish between a "male human being" and a human being in general. Typically, in the New Testament, Jesus is referred to as *anthrōpos* (generally an inclusive

It is apt that the perfect human One who dwelt among us should offer sacrifice and ongoing intercession for His own brothers and sisters, as we learn in Hebrews 2.10–11; yet, like the Father, He is *One*, that is, unique, and He is divine. St Ambrose provides a careful exposition of 1 Timothy 2.5:

> This text indeed refers properly to his incarnation, for our redemption was made by his blood, our pardon comes through his power, our life is secured through his grace. He gives as the Most High; he prays as man. The one is the office of the Creator; the other of a redeemer. Be the gifts as distinct as they may, yet the Giver is one, for it was fitting that our Maker should be our Redeemer.[4]

Another ancient theologian, St Gregory of Nazianzus, in commenting on Hebrews 7, links it with 2 Corinthians 5.15–21 and also with these verses from 1 Timothy when he exclaims: "Yes indeed—what deep significance and humanity it expresses! . . . Even at this moment he is, as man, making representation for my salvation, until he makes me divine by the power of his incarnate manhood. 'As man' I say, because he still has with him the body he assumed, though he is no longer 'regarded as flesh' [2 Cor 5.16]—meaning the bodily experiences, which, sin aside, are ours and his."[5] Indeed, the meaning of this passage in 1 Timothy regarding Jesus' complete humanity is so

---

word for a human), rather than *anēr* (the specific word for a male person), although of course He is both "a human" and "a male human being." In 1 Timothy 2.5, the Mediator is called the *Anthrōpos*, Christ Jesus.

[4]Ambrose, *Of the Christian Faith* 3.2.8 (NPNF² 10:243).

[5]Gregory Nazianzen, Oration 30.14; English translation: Gregory of Nazianzus, *On God and Christ: The Five Theological Orations and Two Letters to Cledonius*, trans. Frederick Williams and Lionel Wickham, Popular Patristics Series 23 (Crestwood, NY: St Vladimir's Seminary Press, 2002), 105.

obvious that it was used in controversy against both Valentinus[6] and Apollinaris,[7] as incontrovertible confirmation of the Church's teachings. The commentator Theodore of Mopsuestia reflects the consensus of the Fathers when he says that this passage in 1 Timothy "refers to the perfect humanity by which salvation is wrought" and then goes on to speak of Jesus' shared humanity with us as the "whole key to salvation."[8]

At the same time, this passage is rightly shown by the Fathers to confirm not only the humanity of Christ, but also His divinity. Several Fathers especially emphasize the divine characteristic of "oneness" that we noted earlier. And so St John Chrysostom teaches us to read carefully, and to notice that the "oneness of God" in this passage is not intended to mark God off from the Mediator (who is also God!), but from idols.[9] The God-Man's divinity, to be sure, is not as apparent to the human eye as His humanity. Accordingly, the blessed Augustine remarks: "For He who was hidden as God was apparent as man. He who was apparent suffered these things. He who was hidden is the very same One who ordered these things. Therefore He saw that all the things were finished which were necessary to be done. . . ."[10]

---

[6]See Tertullian, *On the Flesh of Christ* 15 (ANF 3:534).

[7]Ambrose, *Letters* 27; English translation: *Saint Ambrose: Letters 1–91*, trans. Sr Mary Melchior Beyenka, O.P., Fathers of the Church 26 (Washington, DC: The Catholic University of America Press, 1954), 140.

[8]*Commentary on 1 Timothy* in Theodori Episcopi Mopsuesteni *In Epistolas b. Pauli commentarii*, ed. H. B. Swete, 2 vols. (Cambridge: Cambridge University Press, 1880–1882), 1:88.

[9]Chrysostom, *Homilies on 1 Timothy* 7.41 (NPNF[1] 13:430).

[10]Augustine, *Tractates on John* 119.4; English translation: *Tractates on the Gospel of John, 112–124; Tractates on the First Epistle of John*, trans. John W. Rettig, Fathers of the Church 92 (Washington, DC: The Catholic University of America Press, 2014), 153 (altered for clarity).

Indeed, it is the *humanity, alongside the retained divine nature,* that St Augustine insists is necessary: "[T]he divine Son of God . . . put on humanity without putting off his divinity and built this firm path of faith so that man, by means of the God-Man, could find his way to man's God. . . . For it is as man that he is the Mediator and as man that he is the way."[11] In reflecting on this paradox, St Gregory of Nyssa takes his cue from 1 Timothy 3.16, and calls God the Son's effort for the human household "the mystery of godliness," going on to explain how this ineffable action of God is effective for us:

> By . . . the word *mediator* he reveals to us the whole aim of the mystery of godliness. Now the aim is this. Humanity once revolted through the malice of the enemy, and, brought into bondage to sin, was also alienated from the true Life. After this the Lord of the creature calls back to him his own creature and becomes Man while still remaining God, being both God and man in the entirety of the two separate natures. Thus humanity was indissolubly united to God, the man that is in Christ conducting the work of mediation, to whom, by the firstfruits assumed for us, all the lump is potentially united.[12]

Notice how the saint speaks of the human ailments of *both* sin and death ("bondage to sin," "alienation from . . . life"), and goes on to speak of how we are potentially "united" to the Mediator, who in His own person joins God with perfect humanity. St Gregory's potent insight leads us to understand why we speak of Jesus as the

---

[11]Augustine, *The City of God* 11.2; English translation: *The City of God, Books VIII–XVI*, trans. Gerald G. Walsh, S.J., and Grace Monahan, O.S.U., Fathers of the Church 14 (Washington, DC: The Catholic University of America Press, 1951), 153.

[12]Gregory of Nyssa, *Against Eunomius* 2.12 (NPNF² 5:122), altered for clarity.

true Mediator, and not just as one who accomplished the work of mediation. In His very self He joins together the natures of God and humanity. We might even say that He *is* the *Mediation*—"the Way," as He named Himself. Indeed, the Incarnation is, in its essence, a "mediation"—a tryst, or meeting place where God and humanity are joined.[13] Thus the ascetic Isaac of Nineveh aptly calls Jesus "the Mediator between God and mankind and the Uniter in his two natures."[14] In the same vein, the ancient commentator Theodoret of Cyrus remarks, "Paul calls Christ man exactly because he is the Mediator, the One in whom human and divine natures are joined by friendship."[15]

The Incarnation, however, is not a single instant in time, but encompasses all that Christ accomplished for us, including especially His death on the cross, the most poignant moment of mediation. In the Crucifixion, as the blessed Augustine reminds us, Jesus must be understood both as "the Priest who offers and the Oblation that is offered."[16] But we look to the whole of the Incarnation, and not simply to the cross as the locus of mediation. In the flesh Christ was born, lived, suffered, and died. Momentarily "naked," like every human being after death, He descended to the realms of the dead to

---

[13]For an exploration of this patristic view of the Incarnation, see Edith M. Humphrey, *Ecstasy and Intimacy*, especially chapter Ia.

[14]Isaac of Nineveh, *Ascetical Homilies* 3; St Isaac of Nineveh, *On Ascetical Life*, trans. Mary Hansbury, Popular Patristics Series 11 (Crestwood, NY: St Vladimir's Seminary Press, 1989), 60–61.

[15]Theodoret, *Interpretation of the First Letter to Timothy* (PG 82:797D/798D–799A/800A); English translation: *Ancient Christian Commentary on Scripture, New Testament IX: Colossians, 1–2 Thessalonians, 1–2 Timothy, Titus, Philemon*, ed. Peter J. Gorday (Downers Grove, IL: InterVarsity Press, 2000), 304.

[16]Augustine, *The City of God* 10.20 (FC 14:153).

rob the enemy of his prey, and to raise human beings with Himself as He assumed His risen body.

And there is more! We anticipate not bare rescue from sin and death, as foreshadowed on Easter morning (when those who had been dead were seen walking the streets of Jerusalem, Mt 27.52–53), and as hoped for in the general resurrection. Rather, Jesus' Resurrection is followed by the Ascension, which is indicative of our human journey, and not simply of Jesus' unique divine nature. We know this because when He ascended, He did so by taking the glorified human body with Him as a prize to present before the Father. The Incarnation is not *undone* by the Ascension, but established forever in glory by the One who is our perfect representative, the new and true Human Being. It is not as though our gospel were a cosmic Star Trek episode, where the Captain is "beamed" up and down by Scottie, staging a visit on the planet and then returning as though nothing had happened. No, the whole of our humanity is put on, or "assumed" by God the Son, never to be shed: and it is in this conjunction that the mediation takes place. The Ascension brings the whole matter to perfection. St John Chrysostom speaks eloquently about this in his sermon on the Ascension of our LORD, which has the power to lead us today to great joy:

> What is this? Is the One who is Himself abused the very same One who encourages? Indeed, yes! For He is God and, because of this, our Father, who loves mankind, entreats us. And look what happened! The Son of the One who is making the appeal is the mediator—not a human, nor an angel, nor an archangel, nor anyone of the household slaves.
>
> And what did this Mediator do? The work of a mediator! For it is as if two had been turned away from each other and since they were not willing to talk together, another one comes, and, placing Himself in the middle, loosened the hostility of

each of the two. And this is also what Christ did. God was angry with us, for we were turning away from God, our human-loving Master. Christ, by putting Himself in the middle, exchanged and reconciled each nature to the other. And how did He put Himself in the middle? He Himself took on the punishment that was due to us from the Father and endured both the punishment from there and the reproaches from here.

Do you want to know how He welcomed each? Christ, Paul says, *redeemed us from the curse of the law, having become a curse for us.* You have seen how He received from on high the punishment that had to be borne! Look how also from below He received the insults that had to be borne: *The reproaches of those who reproached You*, Scripture says, *have fallen upon me.* Haven't you seen how He dissolved the enmity, how He did not depart before doing all, both suffering and completing the whole business, until He brought up the one who was both hostile and at war—brought that one up to God Himself, and He made him a friend?[17]

Jesus, then, is both the Mediator and the Mediation, and what He negotiates is not simply a peace treaty, but a new and true alliance by which we become (dare we say it?) the *friends* of God. Only He is capable of such a thorough and deep mediation, the likes of which we could never have imagined. The effects of sin and death are strong; but God's strength, made perfect in the "weakness" of the true Human, is stronger beyond all reckoning. There is one mediator between God and Man, who is both God and Man. In Jesus, we see the answer to the righteous and sober longing of Job, who implies

---

[17]John Chrysostom, *In Ascensionem* (PG 50:444–46). I have not been able to find a published English translation, and so I offer my translation of this astonishing passage.

in his mourning that an adequate mediator between him and the mysterious God must be both human and divine: *For I know that my Redeemer lives, and at the last he will stand upon the earth; and after my skin has been thus destroyed, then from my flesh I shall see God* (Job 19.25–26, RSV); *For I know that an eternal One exists, the One who is upon the earth, and he will deliver me, to raise up my skin* (Job 19.25–26 LXX).

## The Ongoing Mediation

So who is this *One?* We have seen how 1 Timothy establishes the profound blessing provided by the Deliverer who ultimately answers Job's cry and joins together heaven and earth. The book of Hebrews helps us to understand His work more deeply. We are accustomed to calling this book "a letter," and indeed, in its final verses it comes to a conclusion rather like a letter, though without any actual signature. (In the absence of a signature, the author has traditionally been named Paul, and its theology, if not its language, is certainly compatible with Paul's undisputed letters. Yet the actual identity of the author was described as a mystery even by very ancient commentators.) Moreover, in this conclusion the author calls his work a *paraklēsis*—a word of encouragement or exhortation, such as a congregation receives in a sermon. We can thus expect to be encouraged or strengthened as we delve into what this sermon has to say about our Mediator. Especially in Hebrews we learn that, though the saving work of Christ is accomplished in one sense, it is ongoing: *Jesus Christ is the same yesterday, today, and forever* (Heb 13.8). Once a Mediator, always a Mediator. Thus Charles Wesley enthusiastically pictures the ongoing mediating action of Christ in song: "Before the Throne my surety *stands*, my name is written on His hands!"

Hebrews speaks both of what God the Son has done for us and of what He continues to do: this united action is made possible because of the promised union of heaven and earth. The opening verses of Hebrews fasten specifically upon His work of mediation. In this, the age of the New Covenant, God has spoken *through His Son*, because this is the One through whom He created the world (Heb 1.2). This "speaking" through the Son amounts to what we could call a mediation of divine knowledge. As St Clement of Alexandria puts it, Jesus is the *heavenly* teacher of everyone who is created, bringing us to perfection through His teaching, so it is right that we should "Call no one [our] teacher *on earth*."[18] It is perhaps easy for us to gloss over the wonder of this, because we have heard the Gospel so often. But St Anthony the Great (c. AD 251–c. 356) was perceptive when he admonished the monks not to be astonished because an emperor had written to them, but rather because God both wrote the Law for our sake, and now has—far more amazing!—spoken through His own Son.[19] This mediation of knowledge, then, is no light matter.

Besides a mediation of knowledge, the Son alone has also made *purification for sins* (Heb 1.3), thus effecting a mediation of forgiveness, redemption, and sanctification. This is, of course, the major reason for His being named "the one Mediator" in 1 Timothy. This short phrase in Hebrews concerning the mediation of forgiveness, "purification for sins," sets the theme for what we will hear later in the book about His perfect offering, and about the effectiveness of His blood for all time as an "eternal" covenant (9.12; 13.20), *once* offered for forgiveness (9.28) and to make us holy (10.10). From Hebrews we learn that the elaborate system of sacrifice in the Old Testament was intended as a preparation of the people, to teach them their need of redemption, and as a foreshadowing of that which was to come. In Christ we see the one Mediation that provides the actual grounds of

---

[18]Clement of Alexandria, *Stromateis* 6.7 (ANF 2:493).
[19]Athanasius, *Life of Antony* 81 (NPNF² 4:217).

our forgiveness, and that would be eternally available, because it was enacted by One who is both human and divine.

Besides His mediation of knowledge and redemption, the book of Hebrews hints at an even fuller divine work of mediation. Our Mediator has been seated, in the (glorified) flesh, at the right hand of God (1.3), thus joining humanity with God. Here we can be astonished at His mediation of glory and full communion. As Hebrews will exclaim, *How shall we escape if we neglect such a great salvation!* (2.3). Indeed, this mediation of the God-Man means that we have been brought to the verge of a whole new reality, if we have the eyes to see it. Before our imaginations, the climax of Hebrews puts forward a scenario in which we find ourselves in a place far more awe-inspiring than that of the Hebrew people gathered at the foot of Mount Sinai, when the Law was given. We who are in Christ find ourselves at the *true* Mount Zion, ranged with angels dressed in festal garments, together with all the faithful, and together with God (12.22–23). This communion has been made possible by *Jesus, the mediator of a new covenant*, whose blood reconciles, speaking *a better word* than the spilled blood of Abel, which divided the primal household (12.24).

When we look at things in terms of our hope for the last days, we see that Jesus' mediation is the basis for the promised reconciliation of all things in heaven and on earth, and the foundation of our eternal communion with God the Holy Trinity. Mediated knowledge of God is accompanied with mediated forgiveness and cleansing, and will end in mediated communion and glory. It is helpful to note, as some have, that the Greek of Hebrews 1.2 may be translated "He has spoken to us *in* His Son," rather than simply by the instrumental phrase "*by* His Son." After all, it is not a third or foreign party who is the mediator, but God Himself, who is also the perfect Man. Jesus, our brother, is not ashamed to share our humanity (2.11), and so we come, by His mediation, to share in His divine glory (2.10). The very nature of our Mediator, who is both human and divine, shows us that we receive not just forgiveness through Him, but also *a heavenly calling* (Heb 3.1).

Grasping the huge scope of Jesus' work means that we will not freeze the heavenly work of mediation in time, nor fasten it only to the cross, astonishing though that moment of Holy Friday was! Mediation is bound up not only with the Crucifixion, but also with the Incarnation, with the healing and teaching work of Jesus, with the Resurrection, with the Ascension, and with His glorious Second Coming. His mediating work, seen dramatically on the cross, is ongoing, as He *intercedes for us at the right hand of the Father* (Rom 8.34). We anticipate not a static future, but one in which we grow ever closer and closer to God, and more in harmony with the rest of His creatures. Reflecting upon the eschatological vision of St Gregory of Nyssa and St Maximos the Confessor, the contemporary theologian Dumitru Stăniloae beautifully confirms this dynamic picture:

> The souls that at the individual judgment are found capable of communion with God are not fixed in a state of immobile and individual contemplation of the divine essence, but in a communion of love with the Holy Trinity and among themselves. . . . They behold the face of Christ and are not isolated from one another. Together they praise God's glory, and together they serve before the divine throne; and Christ leads them to the source of life, that is, ever deeper in His love, of which they drink without the fountain ever running dry (Rev 7.9–17; 15.2–3). It is not a static contemplation, but a manifestation of love on the part of the righteous and on the part of the Triune God. This communion, even though it is now permanent, always seeks to be deeper, which is proper to communion. This permanent communion at the same time has in itself as communion a movement towards a deeper level, being a "stable movement," or

a "mobile stability," as St Gregory of Nyssa and St Maximos the Confessor say. . . . The basis of this stable movement is God's ever-greater self-offering through His uncreated energies.[20]

## The God Man Who Is Our Mediator

The Fourth Gospel has been, of course, the traditional place where Christians have gone to revel in the divinity of our LORD. Despite the efforts of the Arians in the past, and the confusion of Jehovah's Witnesses in the present (who mistranslate the opening verses of the Gospel) we know that a sober reading of the text, supplemented by a thorough understanding of Greek, yields only one meaning: Jesus is God, though there is even more to the mystery of God than this unique Divine-and-Human Person. The Gospel will go on to unfold the wonders of the Father and the Holy Spirit in due course; the first chapter concentrates upon the Son in relation to the Father. Unfortunately, the proem to John's Gospel has been, for so many, such a potent proof-text of Jesus' divinity that some have not seen its other implications.

So it is that some today assume that the Hebrew people knew all about "the Father" from the Old Testament, and that the primary purpose of the Gospel is therefore to reveal to us the Son. In fact,

---

[20]Dumitru Stăniloae, *The Experience of God: Orthodox Dogmatic Theology, vol. 6, The Fulfillment of Creation*, trans. and ed. Ioan Ioniță (Brookline, MA: Holy Cross Orthodox Press, 2013), 83–84. In the Orthodox Tradition, human beings are understood as capable of receiving God's own "energies," but never God's mysterious "essence," as they grow in holiness. This distinction of "energies" and "essence" enables the Church to speak in terms of the faithful engaged in a process of "theosis" or "deification," without losing sight of the essential difference between the Creator and His redeemed creatures, who are called to be "gods."

this is not the case. The introduction to the Fourth Gospel begins by speaking to us about *the Word* who was *with* or *towards* God (*pros ton theon*), and who *was* God; it ends in verse eighteen by telling us that no one has seen God, except for this Word, who is also *the Light* and the *only-begotten God*, for He is *in the bosom of the Father* and *has told [us] who the Father is* or *exegeted* [Greek, *exegēsato*] *the Father* to us. The very name "Word" (Greek, *Logos*) should have tipped us off from the get-go as to the message of the Gospel. It is by *this* One that any knowledge (*logos*) of the Father is possible. In the Old Testament, God remains somewhat incognito, revealing only a very little about His nature. Through the New Covenant, this One becomes known to us, as the Son shows forth the Father (and then introduces us to the Holy Spirit as a person, rather than simply an amorphous extension of a mysterious God). This revelation of the Father is a special emphasis, then, in John's Gospel, but this teaching is also in harmony with the other Gospels where Jesus is recorded as saying, *No one knows the Son except the Father, and no one knows the Father except the Son, and anyone to whom the Son chooses to reveal Him* (Mt 11.27, cf. Lk 10.22).[21] Here, as in the Fourth Gospel, Jesus appears as the Mediating God.

---

[21]Some may argue that the word "father" is used to describe God in the Old Testament, and so Jesus was not the first to offer this teaching. However, various metaphors were used to describe the unknown God—rock, king, fortress, Adonai or "lord," and husband of Israel, alongside "father." It is not until we know that there is a divine Son that "Father" ceases to be a metaphor among many others, and is revealed to have a mysterious meaning as the first Person of the Holy Trinity. It becomes, indeed, the best name we can offer to Him, as Jesus suggested to us when He addressed Him as "Abba!" and taught us the "Our Father." It is only because of the divine Son that we also can be bold, says St Paul, to address the unseen Father as "Abba!" (Mk 14.36, cf. Rom 8.15; Gal 4.6).

This presentation of Jesus as divine mediator is confirmed by the "I AM" sayings of the Gospel: *I am the living bread that came down from heaven* (Jn 6.51); *I am the light of the world* (8.12); *I am the one who bears witness* (8.18); *I am the door of the sheep* (10.7); *I am the good shepherd* (10.11); *I am the resurrection and the life* (11.25); *I am the way, and the truth, and the life* (14.6); *I am the true vine, and my Father is the vinedresser* (15.1) *I am the vine; you are the branches* (15.5); and then, quite simply (but not so simple!), *Before Abraham was, I AM* (8.58). As with the first verses of the Gospel, each of these phrases, especially the final one, has been taken to underscore the divinity of Jesus. Certainly, life, light, shepherd, vine are all symbols associated with the God of the Old Testament, and they evoke various passages from the Torah, the Psalms, and the Prophets for the knowing reader. Moreover, the "name" revealed to Moses for the LORD is the ineffable "I AM" (YHWH), or in Greek, "the Existing One" (*ho Ōn*). Jesus, then, is implicitly (and sometimes explicitly, in the discourses) claiming continuity with this enlightening, feeding, guiding, tending, and shepherding God who is Being in Himself.

Yet, if we explore the images, we see the element of mediation that is caught up with them as well. He is divine, yes. He is also the *Mediator,* the one who makes a way for us, who is Himself *the* Way. Not only the one who gives living bread, He *is* that Bread, so that those who feed upon Him will share in Him. Not only the one who enlightens everyone coming into the world, He is the Light. He is the Arch-witness who embodies what the Father has been doing, is doing, and will do in our world. He is both the Door, and the Shepherd, poignantly fulfilling the words of Ezekiel, that the LORD will *Himself* shepherd His harried people *and* set up a Shepherd, a new David, for them (Ezek 34.15; 34.23). He is the Way to our resurrection and our transformed life, forging that route painfully by His own death, arising on the third day, and returning in glory to the Father.

He is the very Vine of God, in whom we find our place, and where we will experience the necessary pruning. He is the great I AM, whose delight it was to speak to Moses, to guide the people, and to promise more to come—a time when all would know Him from the least to the greatest.

What Abraham and Moses saw partially, we have seen *in the face of Christ* (2 Cor 4.6). The title by which He is known, the Word, implies this office of mediation—a word carries an idea, a thought, and the authority of the one who is speaking. John's description that closes his rhapsody on the Word confirms this: He is *in the embrace of the Father, and makes Him known* (Jn 1.18). As Jesus says in His poignant words to Philip, *Have I been so long with you for such a long time and you do not know me? The one who has seen me has seen the Father* (Jn 14.9). St Gregory Nazianzen expounds the significance of the Word in a helpful manner:

> He is "Word" [*Logos*], because he is related to the Father as word is to mind, not only by reason of the undisturbed character of his birth, but also through the connection and declaratory function involved in the relationship. One could say too, perhaps, that his relationship is that of definition to term defined, since "word" has the meaning in Greek of "definition." He who has known the Son ("seen" means "known" in that context) has known the Father. The Son is the concise and simple revelation of the Father's nature. . . . Is there anything whose being is not held together by reason [*logos*]?[22]

Yes, there is nothing that can exist that is not dependent upon our one Mediator. The wonder of such dependence is that it leads to maturity rather than leaving us in a state of spiritual infancy. For the Light that

[22]Gregory Nazianzen, Oration 30.20 (PPS 23:109–110).

shines upon us comes to be *in* us; the water that He gives to a person, as He promised Photini, *will become in that one a spring of water welling up to eternal life* (Jn 4.14). His desire is not that we should be only servants, but friends, for He explained that *everything that I have heard from my Father I have made known to you* (Jn 15.15). Thus, we go on from the elementary but staggering lessons of the proem in John 1 to the inconceivable hope that Jesus articulates in His "high priestly" prayer (Jn 17) the night before His Crucifixion. Note that His words to the Father are uttered on behalf not only of the apostles, but for all those who would believe through their witness, and that Jesus describes the unity of the believers and their direct knowledge of God as interconnected:

> I am not praying only for these, but also for those who believe in me through their words, that they may all be one; even as you, Father, are in me, and I in you, that they also may be in us, so that the world may believe that you have sent me. The glory that you have given to me I have given to them, that they may be one even as we are one, I in them and you in me, that they may become perfectly one. . . . Father, I desire that they also, whom you have given to me, may be with me where I am, to behold my glory, which you have given to me in your love for me before the foundation of the world. (John 17.20–24)

The glory, the unity, the love of the Triune God, mysteriously shared between the divine Persons before the foundation of the world, is, by this operative (or effective) prayer of Jesus, to become ours. Jesus' prayer is realized when the gift of the Holy Spirit, the other divine Counselor, comes among God's children, making them one Body, enlivening them so that they can do God's work, reminding them of what they have seen and heard, enlightening them to read all the Scriptures in light of Jesus, God's final Word, and conforming the spirit of each believer to the will of God's Spirit. We receive all this as a gift, not as a right or as a natural and inborn characteristic, for we are creatures, not the Creator—Father, Son, and Holy Spirit. The very same God who insists *I will not give my glory to another* (Is 48.11), now draws us into His fellowship and shares His glory with those who are in Christ. As St Paul reminds the Corinthians, *What do you have that you did not receive?* (1 Cor 4.7). Christ's very nature is to be the mediating God, through whom we receive many treasures. Yet the greatest gift that He mediates is not an external grace, but His very self—which we receive as light, water, life, bread, wisdom, sanctification, redemption, and glory. It is in the spiritual Fourth Gospel to which we have been attending that we hear of the physical water and blood that flowed from Jesus on the cross, just after, for the sake of humankind, He had "given over" His Spirit—or "traditioned" the Spirit, since the noun form of this word is translated as "tradition" (Jn 19.30). He has done all this so that He can truly speak to us, as He did to St Mary Magdalene, about "*my* Father and *your* Father." With Thomas, we cry out, "My LORD and my God!" There is one God, and one Mediator (and one Spirit), whose personal work on our behalf will never end. And one plus one (plus one) makes One.

# CHAPTER 2

# Mediation in the Church: A Family Trait

We have seen that Christians acknowledge and rejoice in one God, who Himself, in the Person of the Son Jesus, is our one great Mediator, drawing us to Himself. Perhaps the greatest mystery about this incomparable and utterly "other" God is that He has "assumed" (or "taken up") humanity to Himself, becoming one with us. Divine greatness is paradoxically seen in God's humility. It can be said, then, both that He will not give His glory to another, and that He wills to share His glory with those of us who participate in His fellowship. In this chapter, we will consider the wonder of prayer, the teaching of Jesus and other scriptural authorities concerning the character of prayer, and the particular gift of intercession in the family of God, or mediation *by asking*, both for Christians and those who do not yet believe. As a first step to understanding how we will share with Him in mediation, let us yet again firmly establish His absolute uniqueness.

### The Otherness of God: A Firm Foundation for Human Mediation

Those who participate in the communion of Christ may reasonably expect to share in some of His characteristics, including, it would seem, the action of mediation, or standing "between" God and others. But this is surely a source of wonder, when we stop to think about it! We might reflect upon the way in which God prepared the human race to understand His coming among us: it is only in the context of a generally established monotheism that the astonishment of the Incarnation could be rightly felt by those who heard the Gospel.[1] Pagans, so accustomed to hearing stories of apotheosis (a human being made into a God, like Heracles/Hercules), and the commingling of gods with humans, would need to be catechized *first* about there being only one true God, before they could receive the doctrine of the Incarnation as the miracle that it truly is.[2] A failure to grasp the utter uniqueness of God is, for example, the major problem

---

[1] This is not to wholly dismiss more recent discussion of first-century Jewish monotheism as including, in some quarters, an elasticity that accounts for the debates concerning "two powers" in heaven, divine language used for mysterious figures such as the Logos/Memra, or Sophia/Chochmah of God, or the status of the divine council. However, the language of "blasphemy" that is so easily adduced in the Fourth Gospel when Jesus is understood as making Himself equal to God shows how a normative, if not always radically unitarian, monotheism prevailed by this time—if not earlier, following the return from exile.

[2] There has been a significant debate concerning whether the word "miracle" is an apt description of God's special intervention in our cosmos, since by the Holy Spirit, He is "everywhere present and fills all things." I am using the term in the popular sense of a mighty and unusual act of God, without necessarily buying into a worldview that thinks in terms of "nature" and "supernature." It is not as though, because of the Fall, God had to move to "plan B" in the Incarnation, and do something contrary to His will, His nature, and the directed flow of history. After all, Colossians 1 speaks of the Son as *always* having the preeminence over the cosmos. However, such acts as we see in the Gospels are startling examples of God's power and supervision, and do not (so far as we can see) fall into the normal category of cause-and-effect that

with modern Mormonism. This religion diminishes the marvel of the God-Man by its teaching that all of us are by nature gods, and need only to realize our potential. Mormonism's counterpart in the ancient world, the Gnostic movement, likewise glorified the "spiritual" person over the "fleshly" and "soul-driven" human; this special category of so-called *pneumatikoi* ("spiritual ones") meant that the uniqueness of Jesus could not be maintained in its varied writings. Nor is the idea of divine humanity limited to Mormonism and Gnosticism. I am reminded of the amusing, but telling, story of Henry Jones, an early twentieth-century philosopher, who was accused of not accepting the divinity of Jesus. His retort was, "*I*, deny the divinity of Christ? I do not deny the divinity of *any* man!"

But Jews and Christians do indeed deny the divinity of humanity, so far as our *nature* is concerned. The stories of Genesis make it very clear that we are created, neither autonomous nor without origin—in distinction to God. In fact, for quite some time Christians recited proto-creeds that stressed the resurrection of the body, but *not* the "immortality of the soul," because in Greek philosophical circles that phrase meant eternal life, stretching out in *both* directions in time, and therefore implying a human soul that had always existed. In contrast, the distinction between God as *Archē*, or "Source," and humanity as derived—indeed, created *ex nihilo* (2 Macc 7.28; Rom 4.17)—is foundational to Christian belief. Without that distinction, the Incarnation would be met with a "ho-hum" response, not with an apt amazement.

I would venture to say that remembering our humble origin in contrast to the eternal God is not instinctive for fallen human beings. I remember distinctly the outrage that I felt as a very young child when I first learned that my parents had a life before I was even

---

we observe in the usual pattern of things. They are thus to be "wondered" at—and "wonder" is the root meaning of "miracle."

conceived—either imaginatively or literally. How dare they! How could there be a world without *me?* The hubris of a child is amusing, but instructive. When we think about life soberly, we should be amazed at even the most common action of the Christian—the fact that we pray. After all, God is by definition all-powerful, all-knowing, and good. Why should our puny efforts make any difference to what He does? He does not *need* our energies. He is perfectly informed about all circumstances, and He will always do what is just and right. Some Christians have suggested, on this basis, that prayer is simply bringing our wills into alignment with God.

## *The Sovereign God Instructs Us to Pray*

But this is not how Jesus describes prayer. And so we must go on to reconsider the nature of prayer, as it is taught in the Scriptures. Jesus describes this human action as *effective*, as something used by God, as do the apostolic witnesses of the New Testament. Prayer is not only an exercise for our spiritual growth (which is an important thing in itself), but something powerful and active in the world around us: this is a major theme in the Scriptures. First, there is the Lord's Prayer, found both in Matthew 6.9–13 and Luke 11.2–4. Certainly, that prayer has other very important elements besides petition: adoration, praise, acknowledgment of God's power, and a request for forgiveness. Those who love God would say that these other elements are, in some ways, more significant for our *theōsis* (our growth in holiness to become like God) than petition is, for they approach God in a disinterested and humble manner. That is, when we give thanks to God and adore Him, we are simply delighting to be in God's company: this is surely a foretaste of the ecstatic communion that we will know when we see Him face-to-face. Indeed, those who are spiritually mature exhibit a transformation of their prayers from a preponderance of petition in the early Christian life, to a later emphasis upon intercession and sacrificial yielding of themselves to the will of God, even when that will is not fully understood. Surely, when all is said and done, we yearn to bear the image of the One who said, *Nevertheless, not what I will, but what You will, Father* (cf. Mk 14.36). In the Christian family, we find ourselves in different stages of spiritual growth, and many of us are particularly grateful for the self-giving and other-directed prayers of monastic men and women who concern themselves with the spiritual and physical needs of others. We also know that the very time such ascetics spend tarrying in God's presence strengthens not only them personally, but the whole Church with whom they are joined. The light that they perceive gives health to us as well, for we are one. And so they mediate not only in their prayers, but by their very lives, as was the case with our LORD.

But the same God-Man who prayed *Not my will* was transparent and realistic enough to also utter the words, *Let this cup pass from me* (Mk 14.36). His pattern of prayer shows us that not simply adoration and acceptance of God's will, but also petition, confession, and intercession are humble activities that recognize the grandeur of God—as well as our human need! Indeed, one can envision God smiling at the ridiculousness of any one of us who consistently prays as though all I want is to enjoy His company, while I am riddled with ailments and fears: He knows when I am putting on airs, and pretending to be more holy than I really am! So it is that the Lord's Prayer, by including supplication, is refreshingly realistic: we are to request "daily bread," guidance ("lead us not into temptation"), and deliverance from evil. Such prayers, since they are addressed in the "we" mode, imply intercession as well as petition. (We can use the term "petition" to cover both of these elements—prayers for me and prayers for others). Indeed, if we were to use the Lord's Prayer as a kind of template (as C. S. Lewis suggests in his *Letters to Malcolm*), we would discover that Jesus' prayer not only includes, but actually accentuates petition, as though that were a main feature of our conversation with God. Obviously, Jesus did not consider supplication to be a grasping or unworthy form of communication with God, or He would not have encouraged us to *ask* for what is on our heart when we address our Father. Moreover, the implication of His teaching is that God will act because we pray.

We see this tendency fleshed out in other places in the Gospels where Jesus enjoins prayer aimed at specific situations: *Pray for those who persecute you* (Mt 5.44); *pray that it [the tribulation] will not happen in wintertime* (Mk 13.18); *pray to . . . the Lord . . . that He will send out laborers into his harvest* (Lk 10.2). Moreover, our prayers are to be consistent and repeated, as He suggests in the parable of the widow and the unjust judge, which He told to His disciples, remarks Luke, to teach them *that they ought always to pray and not become discouraged* (Lk 18.1). In this story, the widow was *asking* for vindication in a court case. Similarly, our prayers are to effect a change, not simply to say "yes" to a future that God has already decreed.

Of course, all this is a great mystery. How can it be that the sovereign, wise, and good God of all things asks for our requests? In terms of logic, it makes no sense, and indeed can be ridiculed. I remember over twenty years ago attending a service in the Anglican cathedral of Vancouver, where the homilist spoke in dismissive terms, suggesting that those who made specific petitions were believing in a kind of "magic." He told a ridiculous story about a man on a ferry with a chicken in a bag. Though I do not remember the details of it, I do remember that the story was intended to rid his parishioners of the naïve idea that our prayers make any mark whatsoever on God's actions. The suggestion was that this mode of prayer is sub-Christian, and dishonoring to the Creator. The rhetorical force of his illustration evoked laughter from the congregation, and may (sadly) have inoculated some impressionable members against the practice of praying for specifics.

Certainly, we have all experienced practices and teachings about prayer that are open to this charge of prayer as magic. One thinks, for example of the "name it and claim it" movement among those who accept the "prosperity gospel," or the cruel assertion of some well-meaning Christians that prayers for healing are not answered because of the person's lack of faith, or lack of persistence. But anyone who takes Jesus' prayer of the unjust judge as a direct description of God's unwillingness to answer our needs, unless we tire Him out, has forfeited the very ground upon which we present our requests—our belief that He is good, and that He loves us. Similarly, there are those who use prayer as though it were a mere talisman, or a means to an end. Mottos like "the family that prays together stays together" have their purpose, but are prone to demoting prayer to an action that we perform for an ulterior motive. The purpose of prayer is, of course, not to "keep the family" together, though it may do that. For prayer, after all, is talking to *God* and listening to Him: nothing could be more significant than this mutual action. Indeed, a conversation with God is unlike any other conversation that we might have, for God is, as the theologians remind us, *totaliter aliter*—totally other than anything or anyone else.[3]

---

[3] This Latin tag appears originally to have come from a story of two medieval German monks who made a bargain that whoever died first would return to the remaining brother to give an idea of what heaven was like. If it was like what they had thought while living, the deceased brother would whisper *taliter*, and if unlike, *aliter*. But what the living monk heard from his reposed friend was *totaliter aliter*—totally other. If this is true of God's heavenly domain, theologians have reasoned, of course it must be eminently true of God: the twentieth-century theologian Karl Barth is, of course, most well-known for issuing this warning, so that we should be reverent before God's holy uniqueness.

## Praying for Everyone

Nevertheless, He has made us in His image, and has called those of us who are in Christ "friends," rather than merely servants. Furthermore, we are commanded to pray, and Christ-directed prayer, as we have seen, includes asking on behalf of ourselves and others. We began the discussion of the last chapter with 1 Timothy's command that we pray for those in authority, even for non-Christians; so Christians routinely and rightly pray even for those presidents and prime ministers who know little, if anything, of God's will. To that injunction we can add other instructions about prayer, spread throughout the New Testament. The Letter to the Ephesians speaks about the necessity to pray *at all times,* and highlights "supplication for all the holy ones" by watchful and persevering prayer in the Spirit (Eph 6.18). The Epistle of James likewise enjoins us: *Therefore confess your sins to one another, and pray for one another, that you may be healed* (Jas 5.16a). What the verse in Ephesians only assumes, James makes explicit: *The prayer of a righteous person has great power in its effects* (Jas 5.16b). Moreover, the letter proceeds to give an illustration from the Old Testament about *Elijah . . . a man of the same nature that we all have* who prayed that rain might cease, and then that it might resume, and was graced by God in receiving what he asked (5.17–18). Conversation between one of God's confidants and the almighty and loving God, we are assured, is powerful.

Petition and intercession vary, both with regards to what is asked, and for whom it is asked. Some prayer is, so to speak, in-house, praying on behalf of other Christians, and for their physical and spiritual well-being. Jesus Himself, in summing up His parable of the unjust judge, promises that God cares about such matters, and to those who doubt God's intent, He both asks (rhetorically) and answers their questions: *And will God not vindicate **those whom He has chosen**, who cry out to Him day and night? Will he delay long concerning their case? I* *tell you, he will vindicate them quickly* (Lk 18.7–8, my emphasis). This conclusion to the parable makes an implicit contrast between God with the unjust judge. Even the judge who is not righteous (that is, he does not care about justice), and who has to be cajoled, will ultimately respond to repeated requests. In contrast, our God is completely concerned with justice, for Righteousness is one of His names, and He will respond speedily. One of His concerns, Jesus tells us, is that His people be "vindicated," or proven to be in the right. We can be assured that this will happen, despite all appearances (martyrdoms, persecutions, illnesses) to the contrary. And we are to *pray* for it, too, not just to assume God will "do His thing."

But why? Why prayer? Well, why did God create us? Does God have *needs*, such as the need to create for the sake of company? No, He is self-sufficient, a completely whole Godhead of divine Persons in communion—Father, Son, and Holy Spirit. Yet, it is in God's nature to create. Perhaps we may envision creation as the deliberate spilling over of His sufficiency, resulting in the marvelous world in which we live—a world that includes human beings who are made (to the astonishment of the angels!) as "bridge" creatures between the other animals and God. He was pleased to make us in His own image, custodians over and members of the physical world, but privy to the secrets of the spiritual world. Indeed, though we naturally divide the spiritual realm from the physical, we are told that Christ aims to *reconcile all things, whether those on earth or in heaven, to Himself* (Col 1.20). In fact, the Incarnation may be seen both as an emblem of this reconciliation, and as the means by which God begins to perform it. God's nature is such that He came to His own, despite our rejection of Him. Moreover, the generosity of God is experienced (at least partially) by all, even by those who refuse to know Him. If God is generous, making His bounty available to others, then part of our bearing the image and likeness of God is that we do good to all—including praying for them, which is the appropriate action of rational creatures who know a loving and powerful God.

Thus, our prayers are aptly (or perhaps, especially!) offered even for those who do not obey Him. In the teaching on the Sermon of the Mount about prayer, Jesus, as we have seen, tells His disciples to pray for those who persecute them. Why? *So that you may be sons of your Father who is in heaven; for He makes His sun arise on those who are evil and on the good, and He sends rain for the just and the unjust* (Mt 5.44–45).[4] We are to pray for others as an echo of the Father's care for all, knowing that *He desires all people to be saved and to come to a knowledge of the truth* (1 Tim 2.4). God has not finished with this world or those who are in it; our prayers are a potent sign of that care, as we express to God what we know to be His will for those who are presently lost. They are also a truthful expression of our creaturely status, for we do not know the trajectory that anyone is on, or what will motivate others to repent: only God knows the heart, and so we direct our prayers about others to Him.

Thus, in praying for those outside the community of faith, we exhibit several Christian characteristics—characteristics that we learn from God Himself. First, we show God's concern and love for all of His creatures; secondly, we honestly admit our need of God's

---

[4]In this translation I retain the literal Greek, *huios* ("son"). This masculine term, used in the Gospels and the Letters to refer to those who are in Christ is sometimes, in the New Testament, supplemented with the term *teknon* ("child"), as can be seen in Romans 8. This dual practice puts to rest any disquiet that the term does not include faithful of both genders. "Son" has two connotations, however, that are not easily captured by the more generic "child"—first, that this person will inherit the Father's wealth, as the eldest son did; secondly, that this person is a small-c "christ" or anointed one, a "son of God" who follows in the path of *the* Son of God.

care and wisdom, and our limited power and knowledge; and finally, our hearts are enlarged, for as we pray for them we find that it is now difficult for us to dismiss them or despise them. After all, in our prayers we have brought them before the One who is, as the Church Fathers put it, "the Lover of Mankind." Looking at the larger picture, we may discern, as our initial passage of 1 Timothy 2 suggests, that prayer acknowledges a hopeful environment for human living, even in a "post-Christian" world. Our prayers put us spiritually in the place of Esther, who interceded for her people, though in a pagan context. Each secular leader is of immense value to God, lovingly made in His image; the leader is also a person with very special responsibilities and considerable powers. Therefore we pray for such persons not only for their own sakes, but for the sake of others who are under their power, and for the sake of the domains that they govern. This may seem challenging when we are praying for immoral or power-hungry leaders. (Even as I write, the Ukraine crisis is upon us!) However, the injunctions in the New Testament to pray for them come from the pens of those who were in no ways naïve, for they lived in the blatantly heartless Roman Empire.

This final insight to pray for political leaders is not simply a practical matter (*that we might live a quiet and peaceful life*, 1 Tim 2.2), but is also tied up with what the Scriptures appear to teach regarding the link between earthly and spiritual powers. Without becoming superstitious, we must acknowledge that the biblical worldview assumes a situation in which things are not only what they seem on the surface. The power that we see wielded by earthly leaders appears to be caught up somehow into a network of powers that/who are unseen. So, Ephesians reminds us that we do not wrestle with flesh and blood, but "spiritual powers" in dark places. So, too, it seems that the nations, as the churches, have their unseen heads: consider the glorious "man" clothed in linen who speaks about the opposition of the "Prince of

Persia," and the aid that he received from Michael, the "chief prince" (Dan 10.13). Following this pattern, we can surmise that those who are in positions of authority have some connection with the spiritual powers. Since they are liable to the influence or even control of demonic and lurking powers, they need our special prayers.

I am not mentioning this connection between earthly leadership and mystery in order to suggest that we ought to speculate about such matters, or to be inordinately afraid. But, as St Paul remarks to the Corinthians, we are given limited insight into the dark realms, and as those enlightened by the Holy Spirit, *We are not ignorant of [Satan's] schemes* (2 Cor 2.11). Simple historical knowledge attests to the connection we are drawing here: Nazism, for example, was not simply a political agenda, but demonstrated an interest in dark mysteries. Other ideologies or anti-Christian ideologues may not exhibit this link in the same obvious way as Hitler, but may still be vulnerable to forces that they do not understand, for they are not under the protection of Christ. They may *think* that their philosophy is of human origin only, but it could well be furthering a nefarious agenda of which they are unaware. The insights of C. S. Lewis in both *The Screwtape Letters* and *That Hideous Strength* are helpful here—the enemy does not require human belief in his existence to exert power over us. Sometimes, indeed, secular people's scorn for mystery may provide the perfect environment for a demonic agenda to take hold. Thus our prayers for those in political power should not be perfunctory, but fervent and perpetual. This is for their sake, for the sake of those whom they govern, for the sake of Christian freedom, and for human society in general.

It is this enjoined prayer, both for those in power and for those who are governed, that demonstrates another characteristic of God— He cares about people and the societies in which they live. Jonah was reminded of this when he did not appreciate God's care for the Ninevites; the prophets show us this as they prophesy not only about

Israel, but about Gentile nations; Jesus exemplifies this when He pours His heart out to rebellious Israel, like a mother desiring to protect her chicks under her wings; Paul remembers this in Romans 13, when he surprisingly tells us that even the secular authority is there by God's permission, to punish wrongdoing. We tend to think about God's concern as only for the individual, or the Church: but God does not, it seems, discount general characteristics of other groups in the human family. He knows the strengths and weaknesses of various tribes, peoples, and nations; though membership in these has no bearing on our identity in Christ, it is still part of the human condition. As those who are the confidants of the Son, we are even given a glimpse of a time when God's bounty will be given *for the healing of the nations*, and when leaders will bring *the glory and honor of the nations* into the New Jerusalem (Rev 22.2; 21.26). In the meantime, the vigor, peacefulness, and equity of the societies in which we live matter—for us as Christians, and for all those around us, especially those who are the most vulnerable.

Prayer, then, is a hallmark of the Christian family, even (or perhaps especially) when it is being offered for those outside the Church, even for those hostile to us. We should have known this from the teaching of the Master in the Sermon on the Mount:

> Love your enemies, bless those who curse you, do good to those who hate you, and pray for those who are spiteful towards you and persecute you, so that you may be sons of your Father who is in heaven: for He makes His sun to rise on the evil and on the good, and sends rain on the just and on the unjust. (Matthew 5.44–46)[5]

---

[5]This is my own translation of the longer variant of this passage replicated in older versions of Matthew, which include three clauses not found in earlier manuscripts (cf. Mt 5.44-46, KJV, and Lk 6.27–28).

The purest and most powerful action of love that we can give towards our enemies is to "bless" them and "pray" for them! Such blessing and praying may come from unwilling Jonahs who, in their first instinct, would like to see the unfaithful fail, and fail spectacularly. As we pray, God will, we hope, change our instincts. But the prayers will never mirror Christ if they are offered in smugness, like the Pharisee (whose prayer was not accepted, while that of the Publican *was*). Indeed, all the good that we know, and the power to do the good to which we have been called are, ultimately, the gift of God—for we, like unbelievers, exhibit unrighteousness on a regular basis. W. H. Auden puts it this way in his startling verse:

> O stand, stand at the window
> As the tears scald and start;
> You shall love your crooked neighbour
> With your crooked heart.[6]

It is the prerogative of the Father, then, to provide the sun and providentially to make it rise, as well as to send the rain that creation can flourish; it is our privilege, as His anointed heirs or "sons" (Mt 5.45) to pray that He does these things, and more, as well. This we do in full knowledge of our own failures! In the praying, indeed, we are brought more into line with God's own character. For it is not His will that we, or they, should perish.

## Praying for Those in the Household

Prayer, then, proceeds on the foundation of an absolutely unique God, who is generous to all, and who invites us to participate in this

---

[6]W. H. Auden, "As I Walked Out One Evening," *Collected Poems* (New York: Vintage, 1991).

generosity when we pray for those outside the household of faith. What of our prayers for each other? The Letter to the Galatians speaks of this as a supremely important act, while also giving us a salutary reminder of our temporality. Even our participation in timely action is important to God: *So, then, as we have this present moment, let us do good things for all, and especially for those who are in the household of faith* (Gal 6.10). The word used to refer to the "present moment," *kairos,* is the same Greek word that is used at the beginning of the Orthodox Liturgy, when the deacon says to the priest, "It is *time* for the Lord to act." Greek also has the word *chronos,* which refers to the ongoing movement of time. Frequently, in the Gospels and the Epistles, emphasis is put upon the time in which we now stand, the present moment—for that is, as humans, what we possess. The past flees away and the future we cannot know: but God has given to us this moment, and has entered into it in His Son, who accepted our human limitations, for our sake.

God, however, is master both of the flow of history, and the precise times. As St Paul puts it: *But when the fullness of time* [chronos] *had come, God sent forth his Son, born of a woman* (Gal 4.4); *For when we were still without strength, at the right time* [kairos] *Christ died for the ungodly* (Rom 5.6). God, then, knows the whole sweep of time, and Himself is the supreme Judge regarding how to act in the moment. We have a certain knowledge of the big picture (shown to us in Holy Scriptures and the Tradition of the Church), and we may also be prompted to act at the right time, through the dwelling of the Holy Spirit among us. This present moment (*kairos*) is ours in which to act, and so we are instructed to *redeem the time* [kairos], *because the days are evil* (Eph 5.16), and reminded that *now is the acceptable time* (*kairos*) to act in harmony with the LORD (2 Cor 6.2, cf. Is 49.8). As Jesus told His disciples before His death, we are no longer servants, but friends, because we know what the Father is doing (Jn 15.15). This insight into our position and our role is not intended to make us arrogant or presumptuous, but to move us to wonder. The Creator of all is including *us* in His love for the world.

Inclusion in this love is expressed in a particularly beautiful way when we pray for each other, further strengthening the connections in the household of faith. Consider what happens when one of us prays for another: that believer, praying in Christ, and through the Holy Spirit, brings his or her brother or sister, with that person's own concerns, before the Father. Here we see true communion: the Holy Trinity, the one being prayed for, the one praying, and his or her concerns (frequently other involved people), are all linked within the give-and-take of prayer. In praying, we acknowledge Christ as the Head of the Body, the power of the Holy Spirit, and the beneficence of the Father, whose will is that we should be one, as the Trinity is one (see Jn 17.21). Recently I was asked to pray for someone in need by a person who had ample reason (humanly speaking) to be angry at the one who was being prayed for. Indeed, the relationship was a tangled one, and involved me as well. Here were the two of us, agreeing to pray together for a person who had a compromised relationship not only with us but with others whom we loved. In prayer, asking God for the good of this person, I found myself overwhelmed at the generosity of the friend who had asked me to pray, despite a chain of injuries caused in the past by the one who was the object of our concern. As I considered the matter, I was further astonished that God could use prayer to bring all of us together, with our complicated histories, into His healing and omniscient presence. The prayer-time itself was for me a powerful icon of the unity to which God aims to lead us. Moreover, it is an *effective* icon that does not simply represent, but expresses and creates this unity. The person at prayer, then, is an icon that is a good in itself, just as marriage not only is a good in itself but it also shows forth the unity of Christ and the Church (Eph 5.31–32).

## Praying in the Assembly

So then, our household is ennobled by personal prayer for each other *in the closet* (Mt 6.6), which is honored by Christ as sincere prayer offered to the Father, without Pharisaic showmanship. We should remember, though, that even personal and secret prayer is not "private," for it involves and embraces others, including, we shall see, the very angels! But there is more. The Church is also characterized by corporate prayer, the prayer of the Body when it is together—an activity as intimate as when "two or three" petition God in agreement, or as grand as when the whole assembly is called to pray on a solemn day. From Old Testament times until today, God's people have prayed together, in small groups, including the family, and in the whole gathered assembly. Of course, it is the assembly of the whole of Israel for prayer that is emphasized in the Old Testament, in the Torah, in the Psalms, in the historical books that call for solemn assemblies. It would seem that smaller groups of pray-ers are taken for granted, and thus not stressed. So in the Old Testament, we see only a few examples of pairs and families praying together: Eli prompts young Samuel's prayer as he comes before the Lord; Hannah desires a child, in agreement with Eli; Naomi encourages Ruth to bless the true God of Israel, and to hope for the response of Boaz; Job "consecrates" his sons with prayer every morning (Job 1.5); Tobias and Sara pray a righteous and faithful prayer for protection on their nuptial night (Tob 8.4–7); in the full text of Esther, Mordecai and Esther pray matching prayers (though they are not together) regarding the safety of the Jewish people (rest of Esth C 1–30).[7] Though the prayers

---

[7]The letters "C" and "D" are used to label the material which is found in extended Esther, lodged between chapters 4 and 5, in the *Lexham English Septuagint* (Bellingham, WA: Lexham Press, 2019), 950–51.

of family and couples are not emphasized in the Old Testament, certainly the mediation of the instructing father towards his son (seen in Proverbs), of the mother's care for her family (Proverbs 31), and of the unity of brothers (Psalm 132.1, LXX) is valorized.[8] Such mediating actions are also registered in the practice of sanctifying and marking the family dwelling with scriptural passages in the Mezuzah (the boxes placed at the entrance of the home). Frequently a tiny piece of paper containing Deuteronomy 11.13–21 was placed there, a passage that concludes with a reference to teaching the family:

> You shall therefore lay up these words of mine in your heart and in your soul; and you shall bind them as a sign upon your hand, and they shall be as frontlets between your eyes. And you shall teach them to your children, talking of them when you are sitting in your house, and when you are walking by the way, and when you lie down, and when you rise. And you shall write them upon the doorposts of your house and upon your gates, that your days and the days of your children may be multiplied in the land which the LORD swore to your fathers to give them, as long as the heavens are above the earth. (Deuteronomy 11.18–21, RSV)

Family teaching and prayers are thus explicitly commanded and assumed. But the major emphasis of the Old Testament is on the prayers of the whole people of God. It is important to remember that the Jewish institution of the "synagogue" means literally "gathering together," as does the Greek word for corporate worship, *synaxis*. The Church Fathers, in discussing Jesus' teaching that He would

---

[8]The numeration for the Old Greek Version (Septuagint; LXX), used by the Orthodox community, differs slightly from the version used in most English translations (based largely on the Masoretic text of the rabbis).

be present among the "two or three" gathered in His name, warned against those who were making the small group programmatic, and thus neglecting the larger assembly. So the fifth-century bishop Peter Chrysologus reprimands those who scorned the larger configuration for worship through a literalistic reading of Jesus' words,[9] and his contemporary St Cyril of Alexandria comments that "it is not the number of those gathered but the strength of their piety and their love of God that is effective."[10] St Cyril, then, did not think of the "two or three" as a prescription for the ideal worship situation, but as an assurance of Christ's presence with us at all times, and of the authority seen in those who are inspired by Christ. Another commentator takes his listeners back to the Old Testament, commenting: "That this harmony of brothers is pleasing to God, the Holy Spirit declared through Solomon, saying, 'There are three things which are pleasing to God and men: harmony of brothers, love of one's neighbors, and the union of man and woman'" (cf. Sir 25.1).[11]

There is one key episode in the Gospels where we see the two and three modeled for us. This is, of course, in the Transfiguration, where Jesus is literally placed *in their midst* (Mt 17.1–8; Mk 9.1–8; Lk 9.28–36). Here the "two" (Moses and Elijah) stand in as representatives of the Old Covenant, and the "three" (Peter, James, and John) represent the apostles of the New Covenant. They gather around Jesus, who shines in their midst, and who suggests a new situation in which God's people will be illumined because He Himself will enact the new "Exodus," the new redemption and exaltation (Lk 9.31). The presence of the two Old Testament and three New Testament

---

[9]Peter Chrysologus, Sermon 132.4–5 (CCL 24b:811–12; FC 17:217–18).

[10]Cyril of Alexandria, Fragment 215 in *Matthäus-Kommentare aus der griechischen Kirche* 224, ed. Joseph Reuss (Berlin: Akademie-Verlag, 1957).

[11]Chromatius, Tractate on Matthew 59.1 in Corpus Christianorum, Series Latina, 9a:492 (Turnhout, Belgium: Brepols, 1953).

leaders reminds us of references in the Law, confirmed in the New
Testament, regarding how to establish the truth of a matter: *A single
witness shall not prevail against a man for any crime, or for any wrong in
connection with any offense that he has committed: only on the evidence of
two witnesses, or three witnesses, shall a charge be sustained* (Deut 19.15,
RSV); *A man who has violated the law of Moses dies without mercy at the
testimony of two or three witnesses* (Heb 10.28, RSV); *Let two or three
prophets speak, and let the others weigh what is said* (1 Cor 14.29, RSV);
*Any charge must be sustained by the evidence of two or three witnesses*
(2 Cor 13.1, RSV). Indeed, Jesus gives the idea of a double or triple witness a firmly theological context when He argues with His detractors
and urges them to receive the truth:

> If I bear witness to myself, my testimony is "not true." Yet there is
> another who bears witness to me, and I know that the testimony
> which he bears concerning me is true. You sent to John, and he
> bore witness to the truth. Not that the testimony which I receive
> is from a human being; but I am saying this so that you may be
> saved! John was a burning and shining lamp, and you were will-
> ing to rejoice for some time in his light. But the testimony which
> I possess is greater than that of John; for the works which the
> Father has granted me to do, the very works which I am perform-
> ing, bear me witness that the Father has sent me. And the Father
> who sent me has Himself borne witness to me. His voice you
> have never heard, and His form you have never seen. Moreover,
> you do not have His word abiding in you, for you do not believe
> Him whom He has sent. You search the Scriptures, because you
> think that in them you have eternal life; but it is these Scriptures
> themselves that bear witness to me. (John 5.31–39)

It would seem, then, that the two or three human witnesses demanded
in Deuteronomy, and ratified in 1 Corinthians and Hebrews, are

intended as reflections of the plurality-in-unity of the true God, who can be seen in Father, in Son, and in the actions of the Holy Spirit, as well as in the human witness of the prophets and the ancient Torah.

It is to such a unified experience of revelation that 2 Peter 1 refers when it enjoins Christians to hearken to the "lamp" of the apostles, whose word confirms, and makes even more certain, the words of the prophets:

> For we did not follow cleverly devised tales when we revealed to you the power and coming of our Lord Jesus Christ, but we were eyewitnesses of His majesty. For when He received honor and glory from God the Father, and the voice was borne to Him by the Majestic Glory, saying "This is my beloved Son, with whom I am well pleased," we heard this voice carried from heaven, for we were with Him on the holy mountain. And we have the prophetic word confirmed. You will do well to pay attention to this as to a lamp shining in the darkness, until the day dawns and the morning star rises in your heart. Of first importance, you must understand this: no prophecy of Scripture is a matter of one's private interpretation, because no prophecy ever came by the will of a human being. Rather, people were carried by the Holy Spirit, and so spoke from God. (2 Peter 1.16–21)

This instruction holds together the importance of mediation and significance of the entire Body of Christ, joining together the "we" of the apostles (the "two or three") with the "you" of the entire community, both in terms of teaching and interpretation, and in terms of direct knowledge of God. The earlier part of this chapter in 2 Peter speaks about Christian progression to full maturity, or deification (*theōsis*): *that you may be partakers of the divine nature* (2 Pet 1.4), and comments that we have *all that we need* (2 Pet 1.3) for this growth. Part

of what we need appears to be the unified apostolic witness of those
who have preceded us.

We have seen, then, that intercessory prayer, as well as mediated
truth, display the character of the Church, as we are invited to participate in God's generous love to all, especially experienced among
His people. Scriptures, which are replete with narrative or stories, do
not simply give us instruction and propositional truth concerning the
importance of mediation in the community. They also give us many
*examples* of the paradox that we have been tracing—how God uses
others to bring us into an intimate relationship with Him, both personally and as a body. We will not be surprised to find that the Acts
of the Apostles provides ample pictures of this marvel.

## The Acts as a Surprising Record of Mediation

Let us consider episodes in the Acts of the Apostles, then, as an early
history of this mediated life, in which God's presence becomes immediate for the faithful. Most notable is its initial description of the early
Church. The community is actually constituted by its being gathered
around the apostles, and around the action of communion: *And they
devoted themselves to the apostles' teaching and fellowship, to the breaking
and prayers of the bread* (Act 2.42).[12] It is with the apostles in their
midst (both for teaching and as the center of life in the community)
and with attention to the Eucharist (by which they see Christ in their

---

[12]For a close analysis of this passage, and the parallelism in the Greek
between the two lines, "teaching and fellowship *of the apostles*" and "breaking
and prayers *of the bread*," see Edith M. Humphrey, *Grand Entrance: Worship on
Earth as In Heaven* (Grand Rapids: Eerdmans, 2006), 50. This may be our earliest indication of what came to be the normative two-part Christian worship
service: first the Word, then the Sacrament.

midst) that the early Christians expressed their faith and grew in it. Those who received the word were dependent upon the apostles for the witness, but the apostles were dependent upon the other believers for the constitution of the full community. The Eucharist, the "breaking of *the* bread," is an apt image of such interdependence—wine and bread made by human hands, blessed in the assembly, and used by God to communicate His saving presence among them. Its very enactment "re-members," or makes present, the work that Jesus performed on the cross, while it also refers the faithful to that great wedding banquet in the last Day, in which all will rejoice in the Bridegroom's presence. Notice that we are not hearing about how the *synaxis*, or gathering, was a means to an end. It is not that they met simply to get "recharged" for the work of being the Church. No, it was something to which they "gave themselves," as an end in itself. Being the Church meant gathering around the apostles, centering instruction and fellowship around those who had been with Jesus, breaking bread and praying with them as Jesus had taught His disciples on that crucial night. Mediation of one to another is the essence of the body, and by it Jesus becomes present with us all, and with each.

Along with positive descriptions of the early followers, the Acts is frank in offering pictures of those whose faith was misguided. Consider the complex case of Simon (Acts 8.5–24), the magician from Samaria, who was baptized and joined the Christian community, but who thought of healing and miracles as a means to an end—the end being his own prowess and power! Both his misunderstanding—that the riches of the Way were for his *own* benefit—and the way that he was corrected show us the importance both of mediation and unmediated access to God. In this episode, the deacon Philip travels from Jerusalem to preach in Samaria. There he astounds many with acts of healing, so that they put away their magical paraphernalia and are baptized. Even Simon, a one-time magical celebrity in his country, follows the wave. However, the presence of the apostles is evidently deemed necessary by God for these new Samaritans to come to the fullness of the faith, and to receive the Holy Spirit. For it is not until Peter and John join Philip, and lay hands upon the newly baptized, that this gift is given, resulting in a parallel "day of Pentecost" for the converts from this half-breed and despised nation (see Jn 4.9; 8.48). They are now one body with the believers in Jerusalem!

Simon, however, is so taken with the phenomena accompanying the Spirit that he covets the "power" of John and Peter, and offers money to have the same gift. (Of course, it is from this episode that we name the sin of "simony," the desire to buy prestige or position in the Church.) The first thing that we may note is that Simon evidently had received "Baptism" only formally, or for dubious reasons— perhaps because he was staggered by Philip's healing abilities, and not because of Jesus and the good news about Him? So then, we receive an implicit lesson—Baptism is not an automatic route to salvation, but must be accompanied by faith. (In the case of infants, those who practice it would say that the child's faith must follow afterwards, being expressed in ongoing repentance, so far as the child is able, life in the Church, and reception of Communion.) Mediated membership is insufficient, but is part of the whole. Peter's rebuke of Simon's request to buy the Spirit and Simon's response to this are also instructive. The apostle explains that Simon's "heart" is not sound, and calls on him to pray in repentance. Simon, apparently uncertain of his own status before God, asks for Peter's prayers. In this interchange we see an emphasis on both the immediate and the mediated. The apostle calls on Simon to pray in repentance; Simon asks for the apostle to pray for him. It is not certain that Simon understands the importance of his own role in all of this: it looks as though he merely wants prayer that he might escape punishment. Peter had intended more for him— repentance leading to a full inclusion in the people of God!

Some exegetes have seized upon this passage as a way of down-playing the importance of Baptism (which evidently did not mechan-ically cure Simon) or Chrismation/confirmation (by which Simon hoped to achieve a magical power). However, Luke has nothing to say about the insufficiency of either Philip's work, or the confirm-ing work of the apostles when they lay on their hands (Acts 8.17). Instead, the problem that is highlighted is the incongruence between these ecclesial acts, and the one who received them. The liturgical acts are not *substitutes* for personal faith, but means by which that faith is passed on and confirmed. Indeed, the Church Fathers, espe-cially the fourth-century St Cyril of Jerusalem and St Gregory of Nyssa who affirm baptismal regeneration (see Titus 3.5), also insist that that belief is fundamentally necessary to Baptism: further, faith must be manifest in works, or else "the water is [nothing but] water." St Gregory thus gives this detailed and pointed instruction to those preparing for Baptism:

It is clear that when wicked characteristics are blotted out from our nature, there is a change for the better. If, then, as the prophet says, "being washed" by this mystic washing our faculty of decision is "purified," "having washed away the wick-ednesses of [our] souls," we became better and were remade for the better. Now if the washing is applied to the body, and the soul has not expunged the stains of the passions, but life after initiation should be on a par with uninitiated life, though it may be daring to say, I will say it and not be deterred, *that in these cases the water is water*, since the gift of the Holy Spirit is nowhere manifest in what takes place, when not only the shame of anger mutilates the divine form, or the passion of greed, and unbridled and unseemly thought, and vanity, and envy, and arrogance, but also things gained by injustice remain with him, and the woman he acquired for himself through adultery serves his pleasures even after this. If these things and the like should similarly surround the life of him who is baptized both before and after, I am unable to see what has been remade, since I see him the same as before. He who has suffered injustice, he who has been falsely accused, he who was thrust out from his own things, in their own case they see no change in him who has been washed.[13]

In speaking of the same matter, St Cyril actually mentions the sad case of Simon Magus:

For although your body might be here, if your mind is not, nothing is gained. Once Simon Magus also entered into the water; he was baptized but not enlightened. And while he plunged his body into the water, he did not enlighten his heart with the Spirit. And his body descended and ascended. But his soul was not buried with Christ, nor raised up.[14]

The personal and the corporate, the immediate and the mediated, are to go together. Simon had no interest in joining the Body of Christ, it seems, but in continuing in his accustomed status within a new community. Luke does not tell us how this story ends. St Cyril of Jerusalem, however, records the prevailing tradition concerning Simon in

---

[13]Gregory of Nyssa, Catechetical Discourse 40.3–4; English translation: *Catechetical Discourse: A Handbook for Catechists*, trans. Ignatius Green, Popular Patristics Series 60 (Yonkers, NY: St Vladimir's Seminary Press, 2019), 154. Cf. *Life of Moses* 2.125–29.

[14]Cyril of Jerusalem, *Procatechesis* 1–2; English translation: *Lectures on the Christian Sacraments: The Procatechesis and the Five Mystagogical Catecheses ascribed to St Cyril of Jerusalem*, trans. Maxwell E. Johnson, Popular Patristics Series 57 (Yonkers, NY: St Vladimir's Seminary Press, 2017), 65.

striking detail (Catecheses 6.14–15), calling him "the inventor of all heresy," numbering him with heretics who depart from the faithful (cf. 1 Jn 2.19), and recounting the sad tale of his pretension to be the eternal Father, who also appeared as the Christ and the Spirit. St Cyril says that an actual cult sprang up from his delusions in Rome, honored by a statue, and Peter and Paul themselves prayed against this, so that his blasphemy was exposed. Yet his godless influence persisted, we are told, in a myriad of new heresies springing from the evil root.

Though Simon's story is not brought to a happy conclusion in Acts (or in ongoing tradition), Luke does relate, amplify, and finish the story of Saul, or Paul's conversion. This story is told three times: in Acts 9, 22, and 26. What is particularly striking to me about the first telling of the story is that Saul, the one who saw the great light of Christ and heard His voice, is sent off for Baptism and instruction at the hands of Ananias and the other Christians in Damascus. The blessed Augustine, in fact, makes this very point when he is talking about the sin of pride, the status of the Church, and the importance of love as its major characteristic. In the preface to his famous tome, *On Doctrine*, he beautifully describes our life together:

> Let us beware of such dangerous temptations of pride, and let us rather consider the fact that the apostle Paul himself, although stricken down and admonished by the voice of God from heaven, was yet sent to a man to receive the sacraments and be admitted into the Church. . . . And without doubt it was possible to have done everything through the instrumentality of angels, but the condition of our race would have been much more degraded if God had not chosen to make use of men as the ministers of His word to their fellow-men. For how could that be true which is written, "The temple of God is holy, which temple ye are," if God gave forth no oracles from His human

temple, but communicated everything that He wished to be taught to men by voices from heaven, or through the ministration of angels? Moreover, love itself, which binds men together in the bond of unity, would have no means of pouring soul into soul, and, as it were, mingling them one with another, if men never learnt anything from their fellow men.[15]

In this section, and in the next two (sections 7 and 8) of St Augustine's preface to *On Doctrine*, he illustrates the importance of our interconnection, and the mediation of human beings in the believing community. He adduces the examples of Cornelius, the Ethiopian eunuch, Moses, and others, and ends with an apt quotation from 1 Corinthians: *What do you have that you did not receive? If, then, you received it, why are you boasting as if it were not a gift?* (1 Cor 4.7). Augustine is shrewd to inform us that our reception of God's truth, and our communion with Him, is not something to make us proud, but something about which we must be grateful. Our reception of God's riches through other human beings prevents pride and shows the elevated status of the "sons of men" that came through Jesus' Incarnation, God's deepest visitation of humanity (cf. Ps 8.5). This mutual reception is also a poignant emblem of the love that we share.

Paul's own thrice-told story in Acts illustrates this matter. Nor does Luke see any grave difference between those things that Saul/Paul experienced in, so to speak, an "immediate" way, and those that he received subsequently through members of the Body of Christ.[16] In Acts 9, we hear about the voice and the light, and how Paul was

---

[15]Augustine, *De Doctrina*, Preface.6 (NPNF[1] 2:520).

[16]Some have assumed, on the analogy of Cephas/Peter, that Saul was renamed Paul at his conversion. This is simply not the case, and he continues to be called "brother Saul" by Judaeans in the Acts of the Apostles. Because of

sent to Ananias to receive Baptism and more instruction. Meanwhile, Ananias was instructed by the LORD to go to Saul and to heal and receive him, since God had great plans for him to instruct the Gentiles in the way. In Acts 22, Paul himself tells the story, while he is defending himself before his murderous countryman. But as he tells the story, the words that the LORD relayed initially to Ananias are included as a part of Ananias' instruction to Paul. The revelation that Paul will be apostle to the Gentiles, then, becomes part of what Ananias passes on to Paul. Finally, in Acts 26, when Paul is telling his story to Festus and Agrippa, the revelation that he is to be an apostle of this sort is simply folded into the initial words of Jesus as Paul encounters Him on the Damascus road:

> And the Lord said, "I am Jesus whom you are persecuting. But rise and stand upon your feet; for I have appeared to you for this purpose, to appoint you to serve and bear witness to the things in which you have seen me and to those in which I will appear to you, delivering you from the people and from the Gentiles— to whom I send you to open their eyes, that they may turn from darkness to light and from the power of Satan to God, that they may receive forgiveness of sins and a place among those who are sanctified by faith in me." (Acts 26.15–18, RSV)

Someone with a mechanical view of biblical revelation might have difficulty with Luke's three different versions of St Paul's story: Did God intimate Paul's future role to Ananias, to Paul through Ananias, or to Paul directly on the Damascus Road? To be sure, the details of Acts 9, 22, and 26 do not strictly match. But they form a coherent and artistic whole, leading to a climax in which the light

---

his "dual citizenship" among Jews and Romans, he has two names, Saul used among the Hebrews, and Paul among the Romans or Greeks.

of God is seen in history, as Paul, even in a Roman prison, commu-nicates the gospel to the Gentiles. It would seem that the evangelist considers that those parts of the mystery mediated by Ananias are *implicit* in Christ's initial connection with Saul, and so can rightly be put directly into the mouth of God by the third telling, once the apostle has lived through the events of his life, as directed by God. They have become his own, and so are rightly understood as God's will communicated personally to him. Certainly, Luke registers no tension between truths received directly, and through others—these are all from the one who is the Word.

A final story in Acts, that of Cornelius and St Peter, illustrates the confluence between different members of the Body who share revela-tion with each other. St Luke, evidently a master in classical writing, recounts the story in Acts 10 by means of a convention well known in ancient novels—that of the double (and matching) vision-report. (This is not, of course, to say that God did not Himself actually use such a parallel visitation for the sake of His Church: what was merely a convention in classical literature becomes a powerful confirmation of God's will in this New Testament book.) Both Cornelius and St Peter are visited by God, and these revelations are orchestrated by the Holy Spirit to bring about God's will of transmitting the gospel to the Gentiles. While St Peter is seeing a vision of unclean animals, Cornelius sees a vision of a pure angel standing within his "impure" Gentile home. St Peter is prepared by *his* vision for the messengers that Cornelius sends, and visits the Gentile, even entering (like the angel in Cornelius' vision) into the Gentile's domain to preach the good news.

We might think that Cornelius is the only beneficiary here—and, of course, he and his family are baptized, receive the Holy Spirit, and enter the Church. But, in fact, St Peter and the other apostles are also enriched in this sharing of revelations. For, before this, St

Peter would have balked at contact with what Jewish law declared "unclean": it would have been difficult, without his shared experience with Cornelius, to know that God had brought about a transformation, so that what was previously unclean could now be declared sacred. And so, he remarks to Cornelius, *Certainly now I perceive that God shows no partiality, but anyone in every nation who fears Him and does what is right is welcome to Him* (Acts 10.34–35). In the next chapter, the apostle relates the story of the intertwined visions to the apostolic council, which then rejoices, concluding, *So, to the Gentiles God has also granted repentance unto life* (Acts 11.18). Cornelius needed St Peter and the Church to tell him the gospel; but St Peter and the apostles needed the experience of Cornelius to understand more fully the will of God. In this story, the Holy Spirit works in the traditional way, from the top down (apostle to convert), but surprisingly overturns our expectations, also bringing about mediation from the bottom up, from Gentile to Jew! As the Virgin Mary prophesied, *He has shown strength with His arm; He has scattered the proud in the imagination of their hearts; He has put down the mighty from their thrones, and exalted those of low degree* (Lk 1.51–52, RSV). The new covenant, then, overturns our expectations, while it also maintains significant continuity with the old. Mediation continues: but sometimes the mediation goes in the opposite direction to what we expected, with the humble mediating for those of a higher "status." The LORD, after all, inhabits each and all of His people, whether of "high" or "low" degree, by human standards.

So far in our study, we have probed the foundational idea that there is one great Mediator, the God-Man Jesus, because of whom human mediation is effective. We have gone on to consider our participation in God's great mercy and love, both as we pray for those outside the Church, and for those within. Our prayers, though personal, are always made within the Body, and so both intimate gatherings and the larger assembly of God's people show this characteristic of God's love as they pray for others. Moreover, the overturning character of the gospel means that we can be surprised at the direction of mediation. Sometimes the "lesser" mediates for the "greater," for we are all interconnected in God's household. It is time, then, to think about the extent of that household, which means moving on to the thorny problem of prayers to the "dead," and the prayers of the departed saints on behalf of the "living." To these issues we turn in our next chapter.

# CHAPTER 3

# Across the Divide: Mediation, the Saints, and all Creation

We have traced the importance of mediation under the New Covenant, discerning the primacy of the mediation of Christ, but also our family practice of mediating one for another. It would seem that the latter is not simply *our habit*, but a characteristic of the Church that is willed by the LORD, who both called St Paul personally, and sent him to Antioch to learn more about this calling. Our God delights to meet us personally, and also frequently uses others in the Christian family to bring us closer to Himself. All Christians, then, deal with the paradox of the startling and immediate God, who has nevertheless planned that we should mediate one for another.

All who name Christ agree that it is right in general to pray for others, and to ask for their prayers. It seems natural to us, though we may not have thought explicitly about this as a given characteristic of the Church, designed by our LORD. But the matter of mediation becomes a flash point in debate among Christians when mediation is interconnected with the doctrine of the communion of saints across the ages (and across the globe). In this longer chapter, then, we must tackle two contentious issues: the lawfulness of our prayers for the departed, and the conviction among traditional Christians that the departed saints intercede for us. (We will consider the role attributed specifically to the Virgin Mary by the historic Church in the next chapter). As we look to biblical and patristic discussions of this double-directioned mediation, we must also trouble-shoot. For our older siblings in the faith, whether apostolic or patristic, teach us how to distinguish between Christian petitions, which assume that God is the ultimate Giver of all good things, and positive thinking, magic, or necromancy.

After attending to these questions, we will extend our discussion of mediation to the mysterious communion that is intimated in Scriptures between humanity and those things both "above" (the angels), as well as "below" (the rest of creation). There are some surprises in store for us when we consider our concourse with the heavenly beings, as described both in Scripture and in ongoing Tradition. As for created objects, there is—connected with the mediation of the saints—the historical role of relics and icons, which have been acknowledged since the earliest Christian centuries as means by which God strengthens His own. Not only faithful words from the saints have been understood as mediating God's grace, but also their holy presence extended into physical things. Many Christians will acknowledge God's use of wine, bread, water, and oil for our physical and spiritual benefit, though even this is a source of debate among some. But relics and icons prove far more troublesome to many, perhaps because they are not bequeathed to us by an explicit command of the LORD. What is the difference between Christian attention to such an object, and a "horcrux" in Harry Potter, or a crystal reverenced by a new-ager? We return again to our questions about miracle and magic. In the end, we will see that mediation, though a quintessential human—and especially Christian—activity extends beyond our own kind, for Christ is reconciling everything, both within creation, and to Himself (Col 1.19–20). But let us begin closer to home, with interhuman mediation.

## Prayers for the Departed: Should We Do It?

In contrast to the squeamishness of some Christians, prayer for the departed seems to be something built into the nature of human beings across cultures. Indeed, maybe that is part of what makes such actions suspect in some Christian quarters—many ancient religions have reverential rites for ancestors, but what if these indicate a sentimental elevation of dead human beings, or a sub-Christian attachment to the human body? Despite this fear, many Christians have thought it natural to mark a grave, adorn it with flowers, and visit it regularly. There are, of course, theological debunkers who would adapt for such mourners the words spoken by the angel to the women at the tomb: "He (or she) is not here! He (or she) is (we hope!) in heaven."

Yet there remains a natural piety that pays attention to the physical body, even among those who see it only as a dear but discarded container for the beloved. The ancient Jewish book Tobit contains a scene in which the angel Raphael praises the human hero and heroine of the narrative for their piety in burying the dead, even at an inconvenient time:

> And so, when you and your daughter-in-law Sarah prayed, I
> brought a reminder of your prayer before the Holy One; and
> when you buried the dead, I was likewise present with you.
> When you did not hesitate to rise and leave your dinner in order
> to go and lay out the dead, your good deed was not hidden from
> me, but I was with you. (Tobit 12.12–13, RSV)

Clearly, then, reverence for the body was considered a significant indication of godliness in the early Jewish community, something

that early Christians shared, since neither group believed in crema-
tion. In fact, if we are inclined to mistrust a writing classed with
the Apocrypha or Deuterocanonical writings,[1] we can note that even
the uncontested Scriptures do not scorn or criticize this natural piety

[1]These writings, in which Tobit is found, were not originally grouped
together in a special section in the older Greek versions of the Bible (Septuagint and other Greek translations), and were typically read by the Jewish and
Christian communities in antiquity, with various assessments regarding their
status. It is not until the time of the Reformation that the Reformers, following the example of later Jewish scholars (after the fall of the Temple), who
excluded them from their holy books, actually extracted these pieces from
their natural generic groupings in the Old Testament and placed them in a
block called the Old Testament "Apocrypha" (literally, those books that are
hidden away). This served as a warning to those who broke from Rome that
these books, from the Reformed perspective, contain questionable material
concerning the "flash points" of the Catholic-Protestant debate, and should
be treated with care. Eventually, of course, Bibles began to be printed without
these books, robbing many in the Christian community of necessary historical
and conceptual material that knits together Old and New Testaments, beautiful poetry, and intimate tales of family life, where women are more front
and center. In the Roman Catholic community, these books, called "Deuterocanonical" (the Second Canon, or Rule), have been used to establish belief
and practice; among enlightened Protestants, they are used for educational
purposes, and as illustrative of piety. Among the Orthodox, who use the Septuagint as a foundation, they are included as part of the Holy Scriptures, and
are called the "Readable" or "Knowable" books, though they would not be
used in isolation to establish debated matters. Indeed, the primary purpose of
the entire Old Testament, in Orthodoxy is to point forward to Jesus (cf. Lk
24.27, 45), and doctrine is established on the basis of New Testament revelation and the apostolic interpretation of the Old Testament, as interpreted by
the Church Fathers. For the Orthodox community, the particular status of,
say, Tobit, or Sirach, is therefore not as serious a matter as it was in the Reformation and Counter-Reformation among Protestants and Catholics.

when it is exemplified throughout the biblical narratives: Abraham's time-consuming and expensive burial of Sarah (Gen 23.1–20); the elaborate mourning, embalming, and burial of Jacob in the Promised Land (Gen 50.1–26); the respectful return of Joseph's remains and their interment at Shechem that forms part of Israel's story (Ex 13.19; Josh 24.32); John the Baptist's disciples burying him with tenderness after his brutal decapitation (Mt 13.12); and, of course, the loving but unnecessary preparations of the myrrh-bearing women on Pascha morning. The angel does not tell them that their spices and preparations are pagan, but only that their ministrations are not appropriate since He is risen. Several centuries later, when Christianity had been well established, St John Chrysostom so fully accepts the ancient virtue of care for the dead (Gr. *kēdemonia*), that he speaks of Jesus as exemplifying "the summit of Divine care for the dead" (that is, towards us "dead" humans) in his commentary on Galatians 2.21.[2] So then, the piety of the women disciples is not in question, nor is concern for those who have died to be relegated to superstition. Christians have never followed the ancient world in declaring *sōma sēma*—"the body is a tomb"—a decaying prison from which the soul thankfully

---

[2]Chrysostom, *Commentary on Galatians* 2:21. For the Greek text, see John Chrysostom, *In epistulam ad Galatas commentarius* (PG 61). Various English translations of Chrysostom's *Homilies on Galatians* (also called "Commentaries") are available, including Gross Alexander's classic translation, NPNF[1] vol. 13 (1889). Many English translators of St John's commentary flatten out the meaning of *kēdemonia* here, and render this simply as "the summit or (crown) of God's care," but the word is far more specific, since it is related to the cognates *kēdemōn* and *kēdeia*. Especially the latter retained its association with care for the dead up to New Testament times, either in the action of mourning, or tending to the body of the beloved. Jesus here is seen as showing the fulfillment of God's righteousness in tending for dead human beings— washing, anointing, loving, and even raising them!

escapes. But are there other ways in which we can help those who have died, beyond ceremonially honoring their bodies?

It is along these lines that C. S. Lewis speaks of the natural impulse to pray for the dead, especially as a Christian who is getting on in years:

> Of course I pray for the dead. The action is so spontaneous, so all but inevitable, that only the most compulsive theological case against it would deter me. And I hardly know how the rest of my prayers would survive if those for the dead were forbidden. At our age the majority of those we love best are dead. What sort of intercourse with God could I have if what I love best were unmentionable to Him?[3]

Lewis's argument here is neither anthropological nor academic: he does not specify in this letter that such an act of devotion is common to humankind. But given what he says elsewhere about there being a universal adherence among human beings to the concept (if not the precise content) of a *Tao*[4] (piety dictated by a moral code), we can imagine him amplifying his remarks to Malcolm with cross-cultural evidence of prayers for those who have died. Moreover, in this letter, he is speaking with his friend about what is spontaneous to him not just as a human, but *as a Christian*, as one who loves God, has communion with God, and loves specific humans—those whom he presumes that God loves even better than he does. Prayer would cease, he suggests, if the ones he loves best were out of court when he spoke

---

[3]C. S. Lewis, *Letters to Malcolm: Chiefly on Prayer*, Letter 20 (London and Glasgow: Collins/Fontana, 1966 [1st ed. 1963]), 109.

[4]C. S. Lewis, *The Abolition of Man: Or, Reflections on Education with Special Reference to the Teaching of English in the Upper Forms of Schools* (New York: HarperOne, 2001 [1st ed. 1944]), passim.

to God: "What sort of intercourse with God could I have if what I love best were unmentionable to Him?"

Though this strikes us as a commonsense approach, we may not take it as a thorough theological answer. It is likely that Lewis decided not to actually write publicly on this topic, but confined it to his personal correspondence with friends, since his "brief," so to speak, was to represent "mere Christianity," and not to dwell on the controversial. So, those who ask may do so with no disrespect: Might Lewis be simply naïve here, unaware of the dangers of succumbing to fallen instinct, or too headstrong to accept corrective Reformed doctrine? Were his prayers for those who had died faithless, or even a vestige of paganism? Elsewhere Lewis says in private correspondence to a friend, "I have never seen any more difficulty about praying for the dead than for the living, and it is quite clear that God wishes us to do that."[5] Well, *is* God's will clear on this point?

We may detect how Lewis would answer by what he says in the course of yet another letter, written this time to his friend Mary Van Deusen. Concerning the communion of saints, Lewis directs us to two passages that are often neglected today—one in the corpus of Paul, and the other associated with Peter. The first concerns Baptism on behalf of the dead (1 Cor 15.29), while the second (1 Pet 3.19–20) speaks of Jesus preaching to *the souls in prison*. Neither of these passages is directly on topic, but may shed some light on our questions. 1 Corinthians 15 reveals the fear of the Corinthians that there is no final resurrection to come, and it offers Paul's instruction concerning Jesus' Resurrection as a pattern that believers will follow, as well as assurance that resurrection is central to Christian teaching. In his

[5]C. S. Lewis, Letter to Rhona Bodle, October 26, 1949 in *The Collected Letters of C. S. Lewis, vol. 2 Books, Broadcasts, and the War, 1931–1949*, ed. Walter Hooper (HarperSanFrancisco, 2004), 989.

encouragement, he uses arguments from history, from nature, and also from liturgical practices at that early time, which obviously included Baptism for those who had died but had not yet fully entered the Church. We do not, for our purposes, need to determine exactly what was going on, except to note that the Mormon practice of being baptized generally for dead ancestors almost certainly was not in view. More likely, the Baptism of which Paul speaks was being performed after the fact because these dear deceased ones had already witnessed to their faith, but not fulfilled it: Perhaps they had been martyred before their catechumenate was complete, or died from another cause in an age when life expectancy was low. Our second passage, 1 Peter 3.19–20, exhibits other concerns. Here, the general topic is that of suffering, and how Jesus' vicarious suffering was followed by His journey to the abode of the dead, where He preached to those who could not hear the good news as the living could. In each case, whether 1 Corinthians 15 or 1 Peter 3, Lewis remarks that the argument "implies that something can be done for the dead." And so, he is emboldened to pray for those whom he loves, on the warrant of these New Testament letters that the dead *can* benefit from what we do.[6]

It appears, then, that the dead can benefit from human action. But what about actual prayers? We may turn to a passage that is at the very least suggestive. In 2 Timothy, Paul (or one of his followers, if we do not accept Pauline authorship of this letter) speaks fondly about the family of Onesiphorus, because he remembers the care and kindness that this man showed him when he was imprisoned in Rome (2 Tim 1.16–18). At the end of the letter, he greets the household of this man, never once speaking to Onesiphorus himself in the letter

---

[6]C. S. Lewis, Letter to Mary Van Deusen, December 28, 1961, in *The Collected Letters of C. S. Lewis, vol. 3: Narnia, Cambridge, and Joy, 1950–1963,* ed. Walter Hooper (HarperSanFrancisco, 2006), 1307.

(2 Tim 4.19). It is natural to interpret these two passages as Paul's memorial for a Christian brother who is now asleep in the LORD, and for whose family Paul cares. Thus, he rightly asks the Lord to *show mercy* to his household (2 Tim 1.16). However, Paul's concern does not end with the family. He finishes his section on Onesiphorus and his family by praying, *may the Lord grant him to find mercy from the Lord on that Day* (2 Tim 1.18, RSV). It is possible, of course, that the brother for whom Paul prays is still living, but in some way "out of commission"—perhaps having abandoned the faith? We might conceive of Paul asking the LORD to have mercy on an apostate Onesiphorus on the basis of that man's kindness to Paul when he was in prison. But if this were the case, then why would not Paul pray more directly for his restoration in this life, rather than for God's clemency to him at the final judgment? It seems much more natural to read Paul's words as referring to one who has departed this life: Paul does not pray for his friend's earthly or present needs (as he does for those who remain in his household), but rather for his reception by God on the last day.

1 Corinthians 15, 1 Peter 3, and 2 Timothy 1 suggest that concern for those who are asleep in the LORD was a natural thing for the New Testament writers. This is not surprising, since we find this practice of praying for those who have died noted in writings both before and after the New Testament. 2 Maccabees, written in the early second century BC, not only records prayers for the forgiveness of those who have died, but explicitly commends this action, perhaps against those who disagreed with it, on the grounds of the hope of the resurrection: *In doing this* [Judas Maccabeus] *acted very well and honorably, taking account of the resurrection. For if he were not expecting that those who had fallen would rise again, it would have been superfluous and foolish to pray for the dead* (2 Macc 12.43–44, RSV). On the other side of the New Testament writings, we find strong evidence for such prayers in

the resting place of early Christians, and also in inscriptions on the walls of the catacombs (second to third century AD). At such sites, we note the request for prayers of those who visit them, or the actual use of prayers to adorn the sites. Most famous of these is the inscription on the grave of Abercius, bishop of Hieropolis, who died in AD 167, which witnesses to a vision of the future glorious Church, and requests prayers from his living Christian brothers and sisters.

As we move a little further along in the history of the Church, we encounter the deathbed request of St Augustine's mother, Monica, that he remember her during the Eucharist.[7] This anecdote shows that naming the departed in prayer during the Divine Liturgy was a well-known tradition among Christians, and not an accretion that came later due to a mistaken idea of piety.[8] Indeed, our earliest extant

---

[7]Augustine, *Confessions* 9.27. See the bibliography for a readable translation by Maria Boulding.

[8]As early as the mid-fourth century, St Cyril of Jerusalem includes such memorials as basic instruction for the newly baptized concerning the Divine Liturgy, even addressing some potential objections: "Next, we make memorial and commemoration of those who have fallen asleep before us, first patriarchs, prophets, apostles, (and) martyrs, so that by their prayers and intercessions God might receive our petition. Next, for the holy fathers and bishops, who have fallen asleep before us, and, in general, for all who have fallen asleep before us, believing great profit will come to the souls for whom the petition is made as this holy and awe-filled sacrifice is being presented. And I want to persuade you by means of an example. For I know many who say, 'How can a soul receive profit after having left this world, either with or without sins, if it is remembered in prayer?' But surely if a king had made exiles out of certain people who had given him offense, and then their relatives wove a crown and offered it to him for those in need of help, would he not give them relief from their punishments? In the same way we also, offering our petitions to God for those who have fallen asleep, although they are sinners, we do not weave crowns, but we offer Christ slaughtered for our sins, propitiating God

"Anaphora" (the part of the Eucharist that begins "Let us lift up our hearts"), dated probably to the third century, speaks about the prayers of the people being joined to that of the angelic host. It then goes on to remember, before the LORD, those who have passed into eternity:

> We offer, Lord, this oblation before thee for the commemoration of all the righteous and just fathers, the prophets, apostles, martyrs, confessors, bishops, priests, ministers, and of all the children of holy Church that are signed with the signing of holy baptism; and us too, Lord, thy humble servants that are gathered together and are standing before thee and have received by tradition the example that has come from thee . . .[9]

Already in the third century, this practice of praying for the deceased faithful is dubbed part of the early tradition of Thanksgiving, going back to Jesus Himself: "[We] have received from tradition this example that has come from Thee." Early and consistent, then, was the Christian practice of praying for those who were asleep in the LORD, not only in personal prayers, but even formally within the Communion service. Moreover, it is ratified by such noteworthy theologians as the blessed Augustine:

---

the lover of mankind both for them and for ourselves." *Mystagogical Catecheses* 5.9–10 (PPS 57:127). For the contemporary reader, Cyril's example of presenting a crown to an offended monarch might seem obscure; his main point is that if a temporal ruler can be propitiated by a present, how much more will the Father heed the prayers of those who are assembled to offer what Christ has accomplished for them, and their departed loved ones.

[9] *The Anaphora of The Holy Apostles Addai and Mari*, in William Macomber, "The Ancient Form of the *Anaphora of the Apostles*," in *East of Byzantium: Syria and Armenia in the Formative Period*, ed. Nina Garsoïan, Thomas Mathews, and Robert Thomson (Washington, DC: Dumbarton Oaks Centre for Byzantine Studies, 1982), 73–88.

For the souls of the pious dead are not separated from the Church, which even now is the kingdom of Christ; otherwise there would be no remembrance made of them at the altar of God in the partaking in the Body of Christ, nor would it do any good in danger to run to baptism, that we might not pass from this life without it.[10]

Today, of course, there are some who would argue that to pray for those who have passed on is incompatible either with God's justice and love—"They are in God's hands, and either do not need or will not be helped by our prayers." But we never make such arguments regarding the living. Are they not also in God's hands, and will not the Judge of all the world do the right thing (Gen 18.25), with or without our prayers? Alongside His omniscience and benevolence towards all, somehow the Holy One includes us in His actions, commanding us to pray for those whom we love—and for our enemies as well. We hold dear both the living and those who are asleep; prayer to the one who loves them most is the very best that we can do for them.

## God of the Living and Not the Dead: Do They Pray for Us?

It is obvious that we, as living ones, have the ability to act in prayer, though we often ask the Holy Spirit and others to help us in this; but what about those who have died? If they are "asleep" in the LORD, can they be aware of *our* situation, or be involved in it? It may be helpful to remember what Jesus said to the Pharisees—*He is not the God of the dead but of the living* (Mt 22.32). But are they actually living *prior* to the resurrection? (Of course, the question may be incoherent as we consider the relationship between time and eternity.) This subject is broached

---

[10]Augustine, *City of God* 20.9 (NPNF[1] 2:430).

directly but mysteriously in the Apocalypse, also known as the book of Revelation—not Revelation*s*, as some fondly imagine, though many things are revealed here. In the sixth chapter, John sees unveiled for him—and then offers to us—the strange sight of those faithful martyrs who have died, and who are resting "under the altar:" *When he opened the fifth seal, I saw under the altar the souls of those who had been slaughtered for the word of God and for the witness they had borne. They cried out with a loud voice, "O Sovereign Lord, holy and true, how long will it be until you judge and avenge our blood on those who dwell upon the earth?"* (6.9–10)

In this visionary scenario, the "dead" are described both as resting, and as active—even to the point of possessing a loud voice. Here they pray for justice—a kind of reverse prayer to what we might expect of the pious, in our tolerant age. That is, they pray for judgment *against* those who are evil and still living, rather than offering prayers to help those in need. This action, though startling to our sensibilities, at least shows that they are not totally dormant: they have a voice, and God listens to it. In response to their plea, they are given a white robe, and they are told to wait patiently for God's timing. It is important to register that the departed saints are not silent, are not ignored, and are not told that justice is none of their business, in contrast to the warnings against judgment that the living faithful are given in the Scriptures. Could it be that "death," or being asleep with the LORD, has brought the kind of clarity to their sight that we do not possess in this life, when we are told that such final judgment is God's purview alone?

### Not Quite an Aside: Judgment, Confession, Forgiveness, and Absolution

I cannot resist pausing at this point to consider the theme of judgment in the Scriptures, and especially in the New Testament. This subject, indeed, is central to our understanding of mediation and the

communion of saints, as should be apparent from the actions of the
saints under the altar. It helps to remember that in English, as well as
in the original Greek of the New Testament, and among the subse-
quent Fathers who used that language, the verb "to judge" (Gr. *krinō*)
and its cognates incorporate various nuances, including discernment
or discrimination, personal criticism or finding fault, labeling, pro-
nouncing a sentence, and condemnation. Thus in the New Testament
we find two contrasting teachings regarding judgment: that this is
the purview of God alone, and that the action of judging is indeed
within the "pay grade" of Church teachers, or even Christians in general. After all, Jesus assured Peter that he possessed the "keys to the
kingdom" for "binding and loosing" (Mt 16.19), breathed the Holy
Spirit upon the apostles with similar instructions about their role
in absolution (Jn 20.22–23), and also extended this role in some way
to believers in general, in the context of personal acts of repentance
and forgiveness (Mt 18.18). Here we find different strands regarding
human authority in tension—a special role given to Peter, a specific
and anointed role given to the Twelve, and a general responsibility in
relation to others, even the "two or three" who agree in prayer. This
lays out a complex *modus operandi* for members of the Church, who
are called both to respond to authority, and to use it, as God permits,
when dealing with brothers and sisters who are in need of correction.

Regarding a *final* judgment, however, it is clear that we have been
instructed (at least this side of death) "not to judge"—that is, not to
pass an absolute judgment on our brothers or sisters, and consign them
to bliss or to separation from God in our own imaginations, or even
worse, in conversation with others. As I complete this manuscript,
I am in mourning not only for the plight of those in Ukraine, but
for the unmeasured rhetoric of incensed Christians who have gone
beyond a critique of certain leaders' actions, to an identification of
such men with the Antichrist. Such formal condemnation sadly has a

well-recognized standing throughout the centuries of Christendom—from the explicit damnations portrayed in Dante's *Inferno,* through Protestant and Catholic vituperations in the Reformation, to today's declarations of apocalyptic fulfillment in newly-identified appearances of the Beast. There is a fine line between acknowledging that "by their fruits you shall know them," and usurping God's omniscient and righteous role. We simply do not know where others ultimately stand before God. Every human being, made in the image of God, is truly mysterious, and is in process, not static.

Both Jesus and the apostle Paul thus warn us: *Do not judge, and you will not be judged; do not condemn, and you will not be condemned* (Lk 6.37); *So do not pronounce judgment before the "time," before the* LORD *comes. It is he who will bring to light what is hidden in darkness and who will disclose the purposes of the heart. Then every person will receive his or her proper praise from God* (1 Cor 4.5). At the same time, both the LORD and St Paul encourage Christians to make informed judgments about actions of people (including ourselves), and they connect this present judging with a future judgment in which it is implied that we *will* participate, not as plaintiffs, but as those who hear the case along with God. In John 7.24, Jesus has been accused by the Pharisees of breaking the law by healing: His answer to them is *not* "you should not be making judgments about who is disobeying God" but rather *make good judgments and stop judging on the surface of things.* The apostle Paul and other New Testament writers call on us to "make proper judgments" about issues, and even to correct (with humility, with love, with deep awareness of our own flaws) our brothers and our sisters. In 1 Corinthians 5, Paul deals with a case of immorality (incest) and tells the Corinthians it is their duty to correct that person, if they truly love him. After all, he says, the time is coming, in the last days, when we shall judge *angels.* Especially within the community of believers, our role is not to let our brothers and sisters go in whatever way they like, but to correct those who are astray—with fear and trembling for ourselves (Jude 23). It is important for our tolerant age to recognize that Paul did not say to the Corinthians, "Well, it's not your business to declare incest as a sin." He argued that since Christians have the mind of Christ, and know God's will for sexuality, they should deal with such a person for his or her own good, for the good order of the Church, and for a bright witness in the world. By extension, when we handle with wisdom, humility, and faithfulness today's transgender or same-sex problems among our own, we are practicing for greater end-time responsibilities.

After all, when we as Christians soberly engage in appropriate "this-age" judging, it is not you or I who decide what is right and wrong: we go upon God's word, and upon how this has been interpreted by Christian teachers through the ages, applying that teaching to ourselves as well as to others who are in our sphere of influence. It is my business, once we are friends, once we have heard and talked about our lives, once we are in an appropriately vulnerable (but not pathologically "co-dependent") two-way relationship with each other, not to deprive my friend of what is true, if I truly care for him or her. And it is my friend's joy and responsibility to do the same for me. In a day that has forgotten about the depth of friendship, we may not realize that even ancient pagans noted the significance of bold honesty as a mark of true friendship, over against mere flattery in a superficial or dishonest relationship (cf. Cicero, *De Amicitia* 24). This characteristic is amplified in Christian communion, as Fr George Parsenios notes in his analysis of the Fourth Gospel, where the disciples are pleased that Jesus is now speaking openly to them (Jn 16.29), and Jesus says that they are no longer servants, but friends (Jn 15.15).[11] Opening the

---

[11]George L. Parsenios, "Confounding Foes and Counseling Friends: *Parrēsia* in the Fourth Gospel and Greco-Roman Philosophy," in *The Prologue of the Gospel of John* (Tübingen: Mohr Siebeck, 2016), 251–72.

heart to each other, even if painful, is part of our calling as brothers and sisters in Christ. How else are we to understand our calling to be "the light of the world?" Like Jesus, we can say, "Look, God has forgiven you! Live a new life for Him!" Of course, this light that we shine must be without a trace of self-righteousness; we must take care of the plank in our own eye, and receive the correction of others as well. As Jesus directed us, *Pay attention to yourselves! If your brother sins, rebuke him, and if he repents, forgive him* (Lk 17.3).

There is, then, a dual danger that lurks in this kind of vulnerable exchange within the Christian family: the general human tendency to criticize others, while minimizing our own sin. Within the Christian context, I might be tempted to disguise these two tendencies from even myself, and to fondly think that I am doing good, when I am actually indulging in pride and causing great harm. For example, under the guise of what some of the Fathers called "discrimination" (which must be governed by humility, and learned from those with wisdom),[12] I might enjoy the feeling of self-importance that accompanies meddling in the life of another, and forget Jesus' warning that I need to remove the log from my own *first*. Just before the reception of Communion, the Orthodox Liturgy prescribes a prayer in which each of us, following the example of St Paul (1 Tim 1.15), considers himself or herself "the chief of sinners." Consideration of others' sins is rightly understood in the Christian Tradition as something to be done in fear and trembling, with great compassion and salutary humility. Extremely helpful here is the warning of the sixth-century ascetic father Abba Dorotheos concerning three increasingly sinful

[12]See, for example, St John Cassian (4th–5th c.), "On the Holy Fathers of Sketis and On Discrimination," *The Philokalia, The Complete Text*, vol. 1 (London: Faber and Faber, 1979), 94–108. In this discourse we see a close association of learned discrimination with patient and loving judgment on the part of those who lead the community.

levels of unrighteous judgment aimed at our neighbor. If we "run down" someone, reduce that person to his or her sin ("s/he is a liar"), or dismiss and hate that one, then our judgment has become a snare or stumbling block to both us and our friend. "Nothing is more serious . . . than judging and despising our neighbor."[13]

The abuse and misuse of authority and of intimate fellowship, however, does not mean that Christians have no calling to be involved in the lives and spiritual health of others. Abba Dorotheos, in explaining how love in the community should work, envisages that, though each of us should be primarily concerned for our own burden of sin, various members of the community have a "charge" to fulfill, for some are called to be "head," "eyes," "mouth," "ear," and "hand," helping to bear the burden of sin in their friends. Those who are leaders, that is, those who fulfill the function of head, eyes, and mouth, learn from those who have come before them, and ultimately from God's own wisdom, how to discern the state of others in such a way as to empathetically help. St Paul, when speaking of the role of the spiritually mature in correcting others (1 Cor 5.3; 6.2), calls this "judgment," whereas Abba Dorotheos (with other later Fathers) tends to reserve the word "judgment" for abusive criticism (though, as noted above, the Greek word for "judgment" contains the idea of discernment). Yet he does speak of the necessary insight of spiritual leaders, who must see and hate the sin, while admonishing, comforting, and restoring the sinner, gently "correcting him when the right moment" comes.[14]

---

[13]Dorotheos, *Discourses* 6.69–78; English translation: Dorotheos of Gaza, *Discourses and Sayings*, trans. Eric P. Wheeler, Cistercian Studies Series 33 (Kalamazoo, MI: Cistercian Publications, 2008), 1977; reprint Collegeville, MN: The Liturgical Press, 131–39.

[14]Dorotheos, *Discourses* 6.76 (Wheeler trans., pp. 136–37).

With St Paul and Abba Dorotheos, we can understand that different members of the community have different responsibilities. Our spiritual leaders are called to account not only for their own actions, but also for those under their protection; mothers and fathers have a duty to correct their children; Christian brothers and sisters, out of love for each other, may also be in a position to help another who has strayed, though such interventions should never be presumptuous, nor take the place of that friend's spiritual advisor. Reminding us of the delicacy of this matter, we have the dual admonition of St Paul, given at the end of Galatians, recalled by Abba Dorotheos, and pertinent to the Church today:

> Brothers, if anyone is caught in any transgression, you spiritual ones should restore him in a spirit of gentleness. Keep watch on yourself, lest you too be tempted. Bear one another's burdens, and in this way fulfill the law of Christ. For if anyone thinks he is something, when he is nothing, he deceives himself. But let each person test his own work. . . . For each of us must bear his own load. (Galatians 6.1–5)

Sometimes, of course, the best "mediation" in which we can engage is to pray for a friend in trouble, and to allow those wiser than we are to bear the burden, rather than thinking that we are "something," and must intervene more actively. The questions that my grown daughter wisely commends to her own children embody the apostle's instructions: Is my word true? Is it kind? Is it necessary? To this we might add, "Is it truly my business?"

Leaving egregious interference aside, we must reckon with the general difficulties that riddle even *godly* interdependence in our contemporary context. Many of us have, after all, been deeply affected by our society, where autonomy and self-direction are considered ideal. And so even my appropriate intervention in someone else's life might seem daunting, while their loving intervention in mine seems simply distasteful. But what is "intervention" other than a form of mediation? For the very word means, quite literally, "coming between." Perhaps if it is practiced as a strictly mutual and equal relationship, the sting might be removed. But, of course, with our various weaknesses and insecurities, even two parties who consider themselves mutually responsible may become ensnared by preening, fawning, power-snatching, or over-dependence. Even a completely symmetrical relationship conceals its own dangers, but we believe that it is worth the "risk."

There is yet another facet of this common life that we must acknowledge, if we are being true to both the Scriptures and to Christian history. Indeed, we have seen this element strongly at play in the discussion of Abba Dorotheos, but examples could be multiplied. While Jesus spoke about "brothers" mutually rebuking, repenting, forgiving, and being forgiven, He also gave particular authority to His apostles to do this work. It is easier for many of us to receive the words, *Confess your sins to one another . . . so that you may be healed* (Jas 5.16) than it is to accept what Jesus said concerning the specific authority of the apostles to forgive (Jn 20.23).[15] It

---

[15]This is not the place to discuss with any detail the complex question of Peter's authority, and whether this is passed down uniquely to the Pope of Rome. Certainly, readers can see Peter acting as a foundational rock (alongside James and others) in the Acts of the Apostles, in a role that Orthodox commentators have described as his being "first among equals." On this see Fr John Meyendorff, *The Primacy of Peter: Essays in Ecclesiology and the Early Church* (Crestwood, NY: St Vladimir's Press, 1992) and Olivier Clément, *You are Peter: An Orthodox Theologian's Reflection on the Exercise of Primal Papacy* (New York: New City Press, 2003). Roman Catholics and Orthodox will, of course, disagree regarding the implications of this for the structure of the Church, whereas Protestants have understood the "rock" to refer only to a faith like Peter's, and do not consider that Jesus' words about Peter's specific

seems that it is a confidence in this particular authority of leaders that eventually led the Church to move from normative confession in the Liturgy before the entire community (some of whom might not have the requisite maturity to hear all sins), to personal Confession before a priest. This tradition of Confession before a leader, however, need not be seen as a replacement for the older practice: mutual repentance and forgiving should never be laid aside, for our sins hurt each other, and full reconciliation requires confession and forgiveness among the parties involved.

It remains the case, though, that the special priestly role of hearing Confession on behalf of Christ, and of speaking and enacting Christ's forgiveness, is a gift that many of us in the Christian community, down through the ages, have received with gratitude. There remains a tension between mutuality and hierarchy (literally, "holy source" or "holy headship") in the Church—a tension that is reflected generally in the idea of mediation, but especially in the Church's practices of Confession. In my own Orthodox tradition, Confession is done out of the *hearing* of others present, but often in a visible rather than hidden place, for penitents have no need to obscure from others, who are also sinners, the fact of their sin. At the beginning of their time together, the priest usually assures the person confessing that he, too, is a sinner, and not worthy in himself; both priest and

---

role have any bearing beyond the first generation of early Christians. To sort this out would take another entire book. I am content at this point to simply point to the tension that we see in Scripture, and in the general Christian Tradition: there is both mutual responsibility among all Christians and a particular responsibility of leaders in the life of the Church—a dual dynamic that we receive from the writings of the New Testament. For more on this "bottom up" and "top down" authority, see Edith M. Humphrey, *Scripture and Tradition: What the Bible Really Says* (Grand Rapids, MI: Baker Academic, 2013), 91–108.

penitent stand in the presence of a holy God, who Himself hears the
Confession which the priest is witnessing. Before articulating his or
her own particular sins, the penitent may acknowledge the Church,
the angels, the saints, and all those against whom offense has been
given, as the priest himself does routinely before the congregation
during the worship service. Then, in most jurisdictions, the absolution given to the penitent is not in the first person ("I forgive") but
in the third person ("God forgives"). Alongside regular Confession
before a priest, each believer includes in his or her daily prayer time
a confession of sin and a plea for mercy. Moreover, Orthodox Christians practice a mutual liturgical confession on the Sunday before
Great Lent. At this poignant time, every member of the congregation
confesses and forgives every other person present—clergy or lay, old
or young. In these ways a balance is kept between the special authority of the pastor and the general authority of all Christians, as they
intervene, with invitation, in each other's lives. Various practices of
confession serve to highlight the mystery of mediation that we are
tackling in this study—God is both immediate and mediated; our
relationships are both mutual and ordered.

We began this discussion of mediating saints "across the divide"
by envisioning, with the seer John, the holy martyrs crying out under
the altar for justice; from this strange scene we have been led to consider other aspects of mediation and forgiveness, order and mutuality, in the life of Christians. But let us move on to our questions
concerning the mediating prayers of those who have gone to be with
the LORD.

## The Elders' Prayers for Us

To the vision of the saints crying out under the altar we must add the
strange image in Revelation of the twenty-four elders, who represent

God's people, who stand before the throne offering bowls of incense, *which are the prayers of the saints* (Rev 5.8). As they offer the prayers, they also worship—for each has a harp. An integral element of worship, though, is intercession, as we have seen already by looking to the earliest anaphora, which brings the faithful saints, by name, before the LORD. Similarly, in the cosmic worship, a particular facet of praising God includes intercession; these twenty-four elders stand between those who have prayed on earth and God, as they offer up to the LORD the sweet-smelling prayers of others. Besides this mediating role of the elders, we see a dramatic example of such intercession, when St John, caught up in the vision, weeps because the scroll is sealed and no one can be found who is able to open it (Rev 5.4). His weeping appears to be a kind of prayer, along the lines of Romans 8.22–26, for he finds himself *in the Spirit on the Lord's day* (Rev 1.10) and has described himself as one who, with others, has been made a "priest" to God (Rev 1.6). As such, when he laments, he represents the praying community that yearns for the restoration of all things (cf. Rom 8.22–24). He is answered (and so are we, as he passes on the vision to us) by one of these elders, who directs him to the Lion of Judah, who is in fact a Lamb (Rev 5.5). John and his readers are answered not directly by *words* from the Lamb, but by the sight of that Lamb to whom the elder points—He is positioned in the center of the universe, and holds in His hands the truth of all things, that sealed scroll that He will open. John sees the Lamb because of the gesture and words of the angel, and we rely on our older sibling John the visionary to mediate this assuring vision to us.

Besides the visionary evidence of Revelation concerning mediation across the divide, there are also cultural traces of this in early Jewish and Christian tradition. Let us pause to note the observers' response to Jesus' cry on the cross, *My God, my God, why have you forsaken me?* Because of the verbal similarities in Aramaic, some of the bystanders believed that He was calling out for Elijah to help Him, to mediate (Mk 15.35; Mt 27.47). Although Jesus is indeed lamenting to *God*, the misinterpretation of His cry is recorded without scorn by the evangelists, and as a natural expression of the cultural expectations of the time. Such expectations on the part of the onlookers are understandable, since they exhibit the same sensibilities that we see in the story of Judas Maccabeus. That martyr for God inspired his troops by relating to them a vision that he received concerning Onias, the righteous priest, and Jeremiah, the righteous prophet, who in their heavenly glory are strengthening the faithful as they go through trials (2 Macc 15.11–16). The concept of the faithful deceased fathers praying for and giving encouragement to those who are in distress is well-established, then, at the turn of the ages, seen in the Jewish book of 2 Maccabees, and this is reflected in the Gospel also.

Indeed, we may move beyond the mistaken understanding of Jesus' words by recalling again that central event in Jesus' own life, where there is concourse between Elijah, Moses, and the incarnate LORD. In our earlier discussion of twos and threes, we saw the importance of this episode, narrated in Mark 9, Matthew 17, and Luke 9. We pause here to notice that Jesus appears to the disciples in a glorious revelation, flanked by Moses (who has died) and Elijah (who was taken up, or assumed, without dying). Lest we think that this is *simply* a symbolic way of showing Jesus' fulfillment of the Law and the Prophets (though it certainly is that as well), we must also account for Luke 9.30–31, which tell us that Jesus spoke with these two heroes about the "Exodus" that He was to accomplish at Jerusalem. Jesus and the two in heaven commune together. Here are two of the Old Testament righteous, strengthening even *the LORD Jesus* for the ordeal that was coming, just as Jesus Himself, both during His life and later in vision, would strengthen His disciples, alerting them to the danger— and the glory—that they were bound to experience (cf. Jn 21.18; Acts

9.16). Peter (or perhaps one of his followers) seems to have taken this act of communing encouragement to heart, for in the Second Epistle, we hear both about the Transfiguration and also about how Peter has made provision that his own voice will be heard after his death, so that Christians might continue to receive apostolic wisdom and follow in it even in times of trial (2 Pet 1.12–15). This same communal mind is demonstrated in the First Letter of John, who reaches across the divide to invite us into an ongoing fellowship. We can see him putting flesh on Jesus' promise that the unity of believers with the Triune God (Father, Son, and Holy Spirit) will be extended to those who will believe because of the mediating witness of His disciples (Jn 17.20). And so, we hear him urge us, too:

> That which was from the beginning, which we have heard, which we have seen with our eyes, which we gazed upon and our hands have touched, concerning the Word of Life (indeed, the Life was revealed, and we have seen Him, and witness to Him and announce to you the eternal Life, which was with the Father and revealed to us!), that which we have seen and heard we proclaim also to you, so that you too may have communion with us; and indeed our communion is with the Father and with His Son Jesus Christ. And we are writing these things so that our joy may be complete. (1 John 1.1–4)

Let us consider carefully the implication of John's words. The apostles have seen and touched, and now bear truthful witness to the one who is the Word and the Life, doing this even to the point of martyrdom (as the Greek word for "I witness," *martyreō,* implies). John makes this formal declaration, using the apostolic "we," and thereby demonstrating the importance of the apostolic community. For we, the readers, are among those who have *not* seen and touched, yet about whom Jesus made His will clear—both to the apostles, before

His death (Jn 17.20), and also after His Resurrection to Thomas—
when He said that those who have not had a physical experience,
but who believe, are "blessed" (Jn 20.29). Jesus turns necessity into a
blessing: the blessing of hearing the witness of others, and exercising
faith as we rely upon them. First, in so believing we have fellowship
with the apostles, who saw and touched: this is, let us remember, the
earliest characteristic of the Church, that they "gave themselves" to
the teaching and communion of the apostles (Acts 2.42). But secondly, through their witness we come to have communion with the
Triune God—with the Father, Son (and Holy Spirit). John slips in
his discourse, it seems, from the apostolic "we" to the communal "we"
when he says that *our* communion," that is the communion of all
Christians, is with the Father and Son (1 Jn 1.3). The result is joy: "our"
joy, which includes those to whom he is writing.[16] And, of course, the
letter itself is a means of mediation. Jesus, to the apostles, to the written word, to us—all this is a conduit of joy and, paradoxically, direct
communion with God. The elder has no sense of dissonance when he
talks both of mediation, and the direct knowledge of God. We see
this in his later words of assurance and explanation:

> I am writing to you, fathers, because you know the one who is
> from the beginning. I am writing to you, young men, because
> you have overcome the evil one. I have written to you, little
> children, because you know the Father. I have written to you,
> fathers, because you know the one who is from the beginning.
> (1 John 2.13–14)

---

[16]There is a variant in some manuscripts that is translated into English as
"your" joy—clearly a scribe wanted to make sure that the reader understood
that the joy applied to them, as well. But the "our" is, in itself, inclusive.

He writes as a witness, yet those who receive his letter *know* God, and they have overcome Satan. In the economy of the kingdom, to those who have, even more will be given. The mediating letter is itself part of what makes the Church's joy complete. So, too, it would seem, are the articulate and compassionate prayers of our older siblings in the faith, who, as the *host of witnesses* (Heb 12) encourage us on. The third-century Church Father Cyprian wrote poignant words to his friend Cornelius, during a time when darkness seemed to be descending upon the world:

> Let us be urgent, with constant groanings and frequent prayers. For these are our heavenly arms, which make us to stand fast and bravely to persevere. These are the spiritual defenses and divine weapons which defend us. Let us remember one another in concord and unanimity. Let us on both sides always pray for one another. Let us relieve burdens and afflictions by mutual love, that if any one of us, by the swiftness of divine condescension, shall go hence [to heaven] the first, our love may continue in the presence of the Lord, and our prayers for our brethren and sisters not cease in the presence of the Father's mercy.[17]

John's stirring letter, along with later writings like that of Cyprian, shows how, by mutual mediation, the Church echoes the tenderness of our Savior, becoming all that God's people are meant to be.

## Mediators Above

We have been thinking about mediation as a particular mark of God's people, a characteristic that is powerful enough to cross the divide between this present life and what we call death. We have

[17]Cyprian, Epistle 56 (ANF 5:192).

seen that it is the long-held Tradition of the Church to pray for those who are, to our eyes, asleep and awaiting the resurrection; and at least some of them, suggests that same holy Tradition, pray for us, encouraging us in our walk. But it would seem that there are others besides human beings involved in this mutual exchange: there have been rumors concerning the heavenly host, which we have heard already in the Apocalypse, though it is not the only book of the Bible, nor the only witness in the Jewish or Christian tradition, to the concourse between humans and angels. To the angels' mysterious, but intriguing participation in our life, we turn.

We should begin by remarking that the Old and New Testament Scriptures are mostly concerned with human life, the human witness to God, and human communion with Him. When angels are mentioned, they are supporting characters in this great drama—and so, though it is a sort of exaggeration, we may speak of these brief notices regarding the angelic hosts as "rumors." After all, the climax of our human story is the Incarnation, when God assumed humanity, becoming all that we were meant to be, both for our repair, and for our fulfillment as those made in the likeness and according to the image of God. There are no lists of angels in the Scriptures such as we might find in some ancient books that are not included in the canon, nor are we told much about the heavenly life that they have with God. Academically speaking, the Bible is not a "mythology" of supernatural beings, since the main burden of the narrative is God's dealings with Adam and Eve, and those who have come from them. By "mythological," academic writers do not mean "untrue," in the colloquial sense of the word, but refer rather to an exalted mode of discourse in which human writers speak of the realities "above" them—whether divine, semi-divine, archetypical, or angelic.[18]

[18]Northrop Frye, in *Anatomy of Criticism* (Princeton, NJ: Princeton University Press, 1957), speaks of several modes of writing, and places the

The Bible, unlike the Greek poet Hesiod's *Theogony* or other mythological compendiums, is not replete with such stories, but includes tantalizing references only where the presence of unseen beings overlaps, from time to time, with the human narrative, and especially with the narrative of God's people. (One example might be the mysterious passage in Daniel 10.13–14, which we noted earlier, where the prophet is visited by a supernatural being who speaks of being delayed by the "Prince of Persia" and helped by "Michael" so that he can finally come to support Daniel.) Most of the time, though, in the Bible the elements of space and time are strong, while eternity and the realms above (and even below) are merely touched upon. While the realm of earth is not entirely sealed or separated from these mysterious "spaces," they generally remain veiled to human sight. Still, in the beginning, God made *the heavens* and the earth—and it is not entirely clear whether "heavens" referred to in this first verse are simply physical, or whether the term also makes a nod to God's hidden realm, with which ours is linked.

Soon in the stories of Genesis, the angels make their brief appearances—in the first place to seal off Eden from fallen humanity, because that easy "walking" with God and the first couple has been marred. Abraham and Sarah, too, are visited by angels, and given the message of God's plan for Isaac. Hagar is given strength and direction by an angel. Jacob sees a vision of angels ascending and descending on a ladder, and wrestles with one of God's representatives—angelic or perhaps the pre-incarnate LORD. An angel appears to Gideon to

-------------------------------------------

mythological above the "high mimetic," or courtly tales. C. S. Lewis, in his *An Experiment in Criticism* (Cambridge University Press, 1988 [1st ed. 1961]), uses a broader definition of "myth," but acknowledges that the kind of story to which he is referring is one that is well represented in the ancient classical tales, and in fact uses one of these (the myth of Cupid and Psyche) in his *Till We Have Faces: A Myth Retold* (Grand Rapids, MI: Eerdmans, 1966 [1st ed. 1956]).

guide him. Moses and the people are guided by an angel throughout their wanderings. Balaam is saved by an angel when he will not heed the donkey's balking. The parents of Samson entertain the angel who tells them of their son's role to come. After David takes a census of Israel, an angel is set to destroy Jerusalem, but God stops him. Elijah is guided and fed by an angel. An angel strikes down the Assyrians, averting disaster upon Judah. The psalms are studded with references to ministering, judging, guiding, and worshipping angels (Psalms 33, 34, 77, 90, 102, 148). Isaiah sees the heavenly worshippers (Is 6) and refers to the role of angels in doing God's will (Is 37.36, 63.9). Daniel is saved from the lion because its mouth is shut by an angel. Zechariah speaks with angels and hears them throughout his vision. Throughout all the "extra" books, accepted as deuterocanonical by some Christians, angels are strongly featured, from the domestic story of Tobit, whose son (with his bride) is guided by an angel and protected, to the visionary works where angels play a stronger role. Finally, lest we think that angels cease to have a function once the New Covenant is established, we see their presence in the Gospels at the Annunciation and Resurrection, and their role mentioned in Paul's letters, the Petrine epistles, Hebrews, and the Apocalypse, where the narrative depends upon them. Angels play a role in our family story, then, though we are not given much information regarding their life apart from us. More often, they are visitors, tasked with something of importance either to a specific member of the household of God, or a turning point in the human narrative—such as their announcement of the Resurrection to the myrrh-bearing women. *Are they not all ministering spirits?* (Heb 1.14).

We have no warrant to get sentimental about these members of God's creation, however. Though they sometimes play a role in domestic matters (*some have entertained angels unawares*, Heb 13.2), the angels are closer than we to the majesty of God, and may not be adopted as "mascots." The reference to their flaming swords in several of the narratives should serve as a warning. Yet we have it on good authority that they are closer to us than we might imagine. Jesus Himself warns those who would scandalize or hurt the fragile among us (children, or perhaps those who are young in faith) that such little ones are of eternal significance, since *their angels always behold the face of my Father* (Mt 18.10). Jesus' words serve as a reminder that *even* the humble have an angelic double, and so are valuable beyond measure to God. By implication, we gather that there are such angelic companions for all the faithful. This conclusion is verified by an episode in Acts, where Peter, who has been imprisoned, is released and comes to knock at the house where his Christian brothers and sisters are worshipping. In her joy and confusion, the young servant-girl Rhoda leaves him standing at the gate, and reports his presence to the company inside, who thinks that it must be *his angel* (Acts 12.12–16). In both the teaching of Jesus and the understanding the early Church, believers are seen to have an angelic representative who stands before God. We can speculate—though not too wildly—concerning what they are doing before God's presence: are they receiving commandments from Him regarding how to care for their human charges; are they advocating for them; are they representing their human counterparts before we actually arrive to join God's divine council and the heavenly worship itself? We are not told what exactly they do, but since they are appointed for each Christian, and stand before God, it is certainly some sort of "go-between" task—a mediating role.

We may be helped in understanding more of this concept by an ancient Jewish novel that became beloved in the Christian community, and that helped to make the name "Aseneth" (Hebrew, "Asenath") common in various Christian cultures, even though that figure is very minor in the book of Genesis, mentioned only three times (Gen 41.45; 41.50; 46.20). These verses in Genesis describe her as the daughter of the pagan priest of On (called Heliopolis in later times, as recorded in the LXX) whom Joseph marries, who becomes the mother of Ephraim and Manasseh, who in turn are the fathers of the "half-tribes." In the romance *Joseph and Aseneth*, though, she becomes a heroine in her own right who repudiates her pagan gods in confession and with ashes, and converts—both because she is besotted with the godly Joseph, and because she comes to have faith in the God of Israel.[19] At the turning point in the story (Chapter 15), she is visited by a shining heavenly "man" who was probably understood in the Jewish community as an angel (cf. Mark 16.5). This heavenly visitor speaks at length with her, unveiling mysteries about how her name is written in the Book of Life, how she has always been intended for Joseph, and how she has an angelic double, called "Repentance," who has always loved her and cared for her. Joseph, it turns out, also has an angelic double—this heavenly messenger himself, who is the chief of God's angelic host, perhaps Michael. Further, the language used to describe Joseph, and also his angelic double, is very messianic. Indeed, the language used by the angel to describe the repentant Aseneth is reminiscent of the apostles' bridal language for the Church—she is "the mother of penitents" and "the walled metropolis for all who take refuge in the Lord" (15.16, cf. Eph 5.31, Rev 21–22). Ancient Jews and Christians who read such novels already had, it seems, a concept of the relationship between angels and the faithful that the author of the novel uses to move along the action, as well as to create a sense of

---

[19]Scholars differ regarding the dating and provenance of this novel. I myself consider it originally a Jewish novel, written probably in the late first century AD, and adopted by the Christian community because of its rich imagery, its concern for Gentiles, and its emphasis upon repentance. For a brief handbook on this fascinating novel, see Edith M. Humphrey, *Joseph and Aseneth*, Guide to Apocrypha and Pseudepigrapha 8 (Sheffield: Sheffield Academic Press, 2000).

mystery. This is not just the story of a good Jewish boy who marries a Gentile girl who must convert so that she is a suitable bride for him. Rather, it becomes a story of every convert brought into the fold of God, and how he or she is drawn there by a guardian angel.

In the common lore of the Jewish and Christian communities, in the stories in Acts, and in the very words of Jesus, then, we hear not merely about the presence, but even the intimacy of at least some angels with the faithful. This mystery is reflected in both the piety and the prayers of the Church in the following centuries. The popular second-century *Shepherd of Hermas* describes angels as those who guard, who protect, who give understanding, and who bring us to repentance. Relevant for our discussion is the strengthening power of an angel to instruct human beings in the art of intercession: "The Lord is abundant in compassion, and gives to those who ask of Him without ceasing. But you have been strengthened by the holy angel, and have received from him such powers of intercession, and are not idle. Then why do you not ask understanding of the Lord, and obtain it from Him?"[20] Presumably the angels can impart to God's people a keen ability to intercede, since this is their natural role before "the face of God," as Jesus put it. What they know, they can teach. This strengthening characteristic of the angelic host may be seen as a kind of subset of their position around the heavenly throne in Revelation 4 and 5. There we see the cherubim *orchestrating* the celestial worship. As the visionary John notes, *Whenever the living creatures give glory and honor and thanks to the One who is seated on the throne, who*

---

[20] *Parable/Similitude* 4[57].4, my own translation. The *Shepherd* is available in various editions (some older translations, like Lightfoot's, are in the public domain and can be found online). Another standard English translation of the *Shepherd of Hermas* is found in *The Apostolic Fathers*, vol. 2, trans. Kirsopp Lake, Loeb Classical Library 25 (Cambridge, MA: Harvard University Press, 1950 [1st ed. 1913]), 1–305.

*lives forever and ever, the twenty-four elders fall prostrate before Him who is seated on the throne and worship Him who lives forever and ever* (Rev 4.9–10). The angels give glory, causing the twenty-four elders to do the same, in their turn. Indeed, it may be this "ordering" function of the angels that St Paul had in mind when he instructed women to keep on their head-coverings in worship, "because of the angels" (1 Cor 11.10) who are conducting the praises of God, from the least of His creatures to the greatest.[21] The angels, as the most experienced worshippers, also have a special concern for intercession, which forms part of our love for God and for others.

It is for this reason, no doubt, that liturgical communities such as the Orthodox pray regularly for the presence of the guardian angels with the faithful. (We should note that our prayers are made not because we think God is unlikely to do something, but in accordance with what we know to be the will of God: our prayers and His will come together in some way that we cannot quite fathom. This is true in every area; we ask, knowing that our heavenly Father cares for us, and will hear us.) As for the help of angels, twice in the Liturgy of St John Chrysostom the priest requests from God what we know He is delighted to give, as the people respond after each prayer "Grant this, O Lord":

[21]Some have thought that St Paul had in mind the possible temptation of angels to lust for human women, glimpsed in Genesis 6.2, and filled out in several pseudepigraphical apocalyptic writings, particularly those associated with Enoch. This seems unlikely, though, since Paul rarely uses the word "angel" to refer to fallen angels. Rather, a remembrance of how angels lead worship, implied also in Isaiah 6, together the knowledge that the angels, in so doing, also "cover" themselves, is a more likely matrix for Paul's brief statement in 1 Corinthians 11.10. For an argument to this effect, see Humphrey, *Scripture and Tradition*, 84–86.

For our deliverance from all affliction, wrath, danger,
and necessity, let us pray to the Lord.

Help us, save us, have mercy on us, and protect us, O
God, by Your grace.

That the whole day may be perfect, holy, peaceful, and
sinless, let us ask the Lord.

*For an angel of peace, a faithful guide, a guardian of our*
*souls and bodies, let us ask the Lord.*

For pardon and remission of our sins and
transgressions, let us ask the Lord.

For that which is good and beneficial for our souls,
and for peace for the world, let us ask the Lord.

That we may complete the remaining time of our life
in peace and repentance, let us ask the Lord.

And let us ask for a Christian end to our life,
peaceful, without shame and suffering, and for a
good defense before the awesome judgment seat
of Christ.

These repeated prayers sum up our human needs, physical and spiritual, not neglecting the present moment, but also looking to the eschaton when we shall see Him face to face. In the course of this corporate litany before God, the faithful are bidden to pray for the blessing of an angel to guide and to guard soul and body.

It seems clear, given what we have seen so far, that there is a strong warrant in Scripture and in the ongoing Tradition for acknowledging angelic care for our souls. After all, Jesus spoke of *joy before the angels of God* over every soul that repents (Lk 15.10). But it is perhaps a little strange to hear a prayer that explicitly commissions the angels with the care of the human body. When angels are seen as helping us to intercede, this makes sense, since they are coming from a position of strength, from worshipping before the face of God. This "work detail" of guarding human bodies, however, seems different. Since an angel has no body (or at least, not a mortal and fragile body like ours),[22] why would care for the human body be *their* task: how can a being with no experience of bodily corruption, weakness, or risk, understand the experience of those who are limited in this way? Perhaps part of the answer is that they are not vulnerable, like us, and so can indeed act as "lifeguards" when there is danger, without fear of drowning with us. But there may be another way of approaching this. We have noted how mediation is not only a "top-down" procedure, but one that is to be mutually practiced among God's people: hierarchs pray for their people, and vice versa. Could it be (and here we tread very lightly) that God entrusts our bodies to the angels so as to expand their experience, so that they will understand something

---

[22]Tradition alternately calls these beings "bodiless" or "light-bodied." St John of Damascus is helpful in holding these two traditions together: "The same is the maker and creator of angels, bringing them out of non-being into being, having created them after his own image as an incorporeal nature, like some spirit or immaterial fire, as the divine David says: 'who makes his angels spirits and his ministers a fiery flame,' describing their lightness, ardor, warmth, extreme sharpness, and acuity with regard to their longing for God and ministry to him and their sublimity and deliverance from all material thought. An angel is therefore a substance that is intellectual, always moving, possessing free will, incorporeal, ministering to God, whose nature has by grace received immortality, and the form and determining of whose essence only the Creator knows. An angel is said to be incorporeal and immaterial in relation to us. For everything in comparison with God, who alone is incomparable, is dense and material, for only the divine is truly immaterial and incorporeal." *On the Orthodox Faith* (=*Exact Exposition*) 17 (PPS 62:99). In our own day, C. S. Lewis gives rise to similar speculation concerning the makeup of angelic bodies in his Space Trilogy, where sometimes the Eldila are visible as light, but sometimes hidden.

about what it is to be human, and not by nature powerful as they are? Is their concourse with us as much for their sake as for ours?

This is, of course, speculative, but it seems to be in harmony with what we see elsewhere regarding the limitations of angels, and how human beings in Christ can "instruct" or "show" them things that are beyond the angels' own immediate knowledge. In Ephesians, where the apostle is confessing his own weakness, coupled with his calling, we hear these astonishing words:

> Of this gospel I was made a servant according to the gift of God's grace, given to me by the energy of His power. To me, though I am the least of all the saints, this grace was given, to announce to the nations the inscrutable wealth of Christ, and to bring to light for everyone the plan of the mystery hidden from the ages in God, the creator of all, *so that now through the Church the many-colored wisdom of God might be made known to the principalities and powers in the heavenly places.* This was according to the ages-old purpose that He accomplished in Christ Jesus our Lord. (Ephesians 3.7–11)

That statement is even more startling than the insight that fleshless creatures might hold a concern for the human body. Here it is the Church, human beings, who are called to show forth the gospel to the angels—to angels in heaven, not the fallen ones! God's wisdom is variegated, "many-colored," and can be aptly shown by different parts of His creation—including those who are "the least" and who possess a weak human body. The apostle recognizes his own weakness, and also, it seems, stands amazed at God's commissioning of the Church, the Body of Christ, to witness to the very powers of heaven.

After all, though we are subjected to death, we have been raised up with Christ in heavenly places (Eph 2.5–6), and so can witness to the resurrection of the body. We can make this declaration because we have the risen Christ in mind, but also because He has told us about the glory that awaits us. Like the woman who washed Jesus' feet, much has been forgiven and restored to us, and so we love much: with this overflowing gratitude we can profess God's love to those cosmic beings who have not been subject to sin or death. God the Son took on a *human* body, not an angelic one, for the salvation of the cosmos; thus it is that we know, more innately than the faithful angels, who have never taken on flesh or death, who it is that He became for our sake. The witness of human beings is integral to the reconciliation of the world, since God became human. In terms of *inner* knowledge, we are well placed to "go between," to mediate this aspect of God's glory, to the angels. At present, though, we mostly *receive* from them gladly, since for now they are stronger and less mercurial members of God's household. The wise St John Climacus reminds us: "Let it not be a surprise to you that [you] stumble each day. Never give up, but hold your ground with courage. Most assuredly, your guardian angel will give honor to your long-suffering."[23] At the same time, we minister to them, displaying the glory of Jesus in human bodies.

Finally, our ministry to angels includes a dark side. St Paul assures us that we will be brought to a position in which we can actually "judge" angels (1 Cor 6.3)—that, is, the fallen ones, who are also depicted in a judgment scene with the righteous Enoch in several extra-biblical writings. This kind of judicial mediation that St Paul envisages is similar in logic to the words that Jesus speaks about the Gentile communities and leaders that will rise up against

---

[23]John Climacus, *The Ladder of Divine Ascent* 5.30; English translation: John Climacus, *The Ladder of Divine Ascent*, rev. ed., trans. Archimandrite Lazarus Moore (Brookline, MA: Holy Transfiguration Monastery, 2019 [1st ed. 1959]), 106.

His generation, because, weak though they were, they listened to the preaching of the prophets, whereas Jesus has been ignored by many of His compatriots (Mt 12.41–42). It is God's own historical people, Israel, that should have the potential to judge, according to Jesus' scenario, but they are replaced, it seems, by Gentiles, weaker members of the human community. Similarly, on the cosmic level, it is Lucifer, the original "Light-bearer" and his powerful spirit-companions who should see things as they are, but they will be spoken against at the end by redeemed human beings! Occasionally, mediation delivers judgment and not blessing.

At the end, then, human beings will take their rightful places beside the LORD, praising Him, and even judging—ours is a role that eventually will surpass that of the angels, it seems. Even before the last days, there are some places, described in the Psalms, where human beings, perhaps with some holy impudence, take on the role of exhorting the angels. Throughout the Psalms there are scattered injunctions to the whole cosmos to "praise the LORD," articulated by David (or the other psalmists), and therefore also by the community that takes these encouraging psalms on its lips. One example would be Psalm 103 (LXX 102), where the human worshipper calls upon all the elements of the cosmos to praise the LORD, beginning with himself or herself:

> Bless the LORD, O my soul: and all that is within me,
> bless his holy name.
> Bless the LORD, O my soul, and forget not all his
> benefits:
> who forgiveth all thine iniquities;
> who healeth all thy diseases;
> who redeemeth thy life from destruction;
> who crowneth thee with lovingkindness and tender
> mercies;

who satisfieth thy mouth with good things; so that

thy youth is renewed like the eagle's. . . .

For as the heaven is high above the earth, so great is

his mercy toward them that fear him.

As far as the east is from the west, so far hath he

removed our transgressions from us.

Like as a father pitieth his children, so the LORD

pitieth them that fear him.

For he knoweth our frame; he remembereth that we

are dust. . . .

The LORD hath prepared his throne in the heavens;

and his kingdom ruleth over all.

Bless the LORD, ye his angels, that excel in strength,

that do his commandments, hearkening unto the

voice of his word.

Bless ye the LORD, all ye his hosts; ye ministers of his,

that do his pleasure.

Bless the LORD, all his works in all places of his

dominion:

bless the LORD, O my soul. (KJV)

There is a bold logic to psalms like this. It is not enough for me to praise the LORD on my own, but with the Psalmist, we *all* cry to the *whole* cosmos, that which is "above" as well as "below" us, to join in the worship. The exuberance of praise leads us to reach above, and to call out, as in the Western hymn *Praise My Soul, the King of Heaven:* "Angels, help us to adore Him! Ye behold Him face to face!" When we are looking to the LORD, such holy audacity, reaching forward to our final place in God's plan, is natural. As Clement of Alexandria explains, when we are caught up in our prayers, the "divide" is blurred, and we worship together with them: "The one who is intimate with God also prays in the society of angels, as being already of angelic rank, and he is never out of their holy keeping; and though he pray alone, he has the choir of saints standing with him."[24] Sometimes, surprisingly, we mediate *for* these shining beings, as well as praying alongside them.

## Mediation Below

These very psalms and hymns in which we enjoin the heavenly powers to worship with us also provide the creation "below" us with a human voice. Besides Psalm 102 (LXX) and the final psalms of the Bible, there is also the *Song of the Three*, a canticle that has been beloved from the earliest centuries in the Church. In the Septuagint, it appears in the context of the persecution of Daniel and his three friends who sing in the furnace, but in most English Bibles it has been included in the Apocrypha as a separate piece. As the three young men in the fiery furnace exalt God, they fold into their praise the adoration of the entire cosmos: alongside the angels above, the heavenly bodies and water, the winds and rains, all the elements, all the seasons, night and day, all growing things, all the birds, all the animals, all humanity, and all the persecuted faithful (personified by the three in the furnace). The hymn has the form of a "bidding" prayer, with each element of creation called upon to praise, followed by the antiphonal refrain "Sing praise to Him and highly exalt Him forever," which gives the sense of each part of creation joining in, as asked. Such an expansive song led by God's people places us within a vibrant universe that is praising the LORD, in its teeming variety. Without joining in the entire song, some of the effect is lost, but this is a taste of it:

> Blessed art thou, O Lord, God of our fathers,
> and to be praised and highly exalted for ever. . . .

[24]Clement of Alexandria, *Miscellanies (Stromata)* 7.12 (ANF 2:545).

Bless the Lord, all works of the Lord,

sing praise to him and highly exalt him for ever.

Bless the Lord, you heavens,

sing praise to him and highly exalt him for ever.

Bless the Lord, you angels of the Lord,

sing praise to him and highly exalt him for ever.

Bless the Lord, all waters above the heaven,

sing praise to him and highly exalt him for ever.

Bless the Lord, all powers,

sing praise to him and highly exalt him for ever.

Bless the Lord, sun and moon,

sing praise to him and highly exalt him for ever.

Bless the Lord, stars of heaven,

sing praise to him and highly exalt him for ever.

Bless the Lord, all rain and dew,

sing praise to him and highly exalt him for ever.

Bless the Lord, all winds,

sing praise to him and highly exalt him for ever. . . .

Bless the Lord, you sons of men,

sing praise to him and highly exalt him for ever.

Bless the Lord, O Israel,

sing praise to him and highly exalt him for ever.

Bless the Lord, you priests of the Lord,

sing praise to him and highly exalt him for ever.

Bless the Lord, you servants of the Lord,

sing praise to him and highly exalt him for ever.

Bless the Lord, spirits and souls of the righteous,

sing praise to him and highly exalt him for ever.

Bless the Lord, you who are holy and humble in
    heart,

sing praise to him and highly exalt him for ever.

> Bless the Lord, Hananiah, Azariah, and Mishael,
> sing praise to him and highly exalt him for ever;
> for he has rescued us from Hades and saved us from
>     the hand of death, and delivered us from the
>     midst of the burning fiery furnace; from the
>     midst of the fire he has delivered us.
> Give thanks to the Lord, for he is good,
> for his mercy endures for ever.
> Bless him, all who worship the Lord, the God of gods,
> sing praise to him and give thanks to him,
> for his mercy endures for ever.
> (*Song of the Three,* RSV Apocrypha)

While singing, the three friends of Daniel—Hananiah, Azariah, and Mishael (often better-known by their Babylonian names: Shadrach, Meshach, and Abednego)—walk in the furnace because they refuse to be idolaters. As they sing in the flames, Azariah confesses that the Hebrew people are exiled because of God's righteous judgment. Then the angel of the Lord expels the burning flame and makes the interior of the furnace like a moist wind. Later generations of Christians saw this "angel" as a pre-incarnational appearance of the Son, the very personification of God's great Mercy, which is the main theme of the song: *His mercy endures forever!* With one voice the men praise God the Creator, call upon every part of the cosmos to bless and praise God, and end by admonishing themselves to praise the LORD who has rescued them from Hell and death. All this is sung as they *give thanks to the LORD, for he is good, for his mercy endures forever.*

They are, of course, celebrating the creative power of God, who is *alone. . . glorious over the whole world,* and remembering the beginning of His works. But besides enumerating all the things that God has created, the song also calls on each of these elements to give praise. As human beings, made in the image of God, the three exuberantly echo the mercy, fullness, and joy of the Creator, and they present a picture of the world before our eyes. Even in the region of fire, where life is at the margins, God reaches them and puts praise in their mouth. They have been exiled by the pagan king from the expanse of this world, and are closed up in a furnace that threatens to dissolve them: even here, they produce for those who hear and enter into their psalm, a vivid image. We see, through their words, a cosmos as high as the cherubim and the firmament of heavens, as deep as the rivers and the sporting sea creatures, as wild as the beasts, and as sophisticated as some human nations. By their worship, God's own humble servants instruct all the works of the Lord to praise and bless Him. After all, that is what the cosmos has been called to do, through the very blessing of life. We see these young men, then, assuming the role of priests between creation and God, and enabling those elements that have no voice of their own to offer praise. We, too, are drawn by their song into thanksgiving. (Recall that the Latin word for priest, *pontifex*, means quite literally "bridge-builder.") When we sing such a psalm, we also become artists, little creators *under* the great Creator, together depicting God's world, encouraging it to worship, and bringing our song, the world, and ourselves into God's presence with thanksgiving.

This kind of cosmic thanksgiving is consonant, indeed, with what we do in the "Eucharist," which literally means the "Thanksgiving." We gratefully offer to God bread that we have made from the wheat that has been grown with His help, and wine that comes from the plants that He has made to grow, and that we have cultivated. These physical objects, touched by our hands, along with the oil of healing, are used by God not only to bring us blessing, but to bring us into communion with Him. The same holds true for water, which we do nothing to produce, but which we must collect and guard for God's purposes of cleansing and Baptism. C. S. Lewis goes so far as to say that our LORD uses matter "to put the God-life in us!"[25] Do we see what is happening? Yes, our hands have touched and offer these things to God, showing our God-given potential to "bless God" with our offering, as He wills it. But it is also the case that these created elements *mediate* God to us in a divinely intended manner. Jesus gave the command to use these things—water to cleanse and unite us to Christ and each other, bread and wine as the "medicine of immortality."[26] Similarly, we are enjoined by the apostle to use oil for healing in the Church (Jas 5.14), a practice already attested in the Gospels during the ministry of the Twelve (Mk 6.13). Material things actually participate in our actions of mediation. We offer them to God, and God blesses us through them. As St Basil's Liturgy puts it, when offered by us and used by God, they are revealed for what they are— vehicles of the very blessing of God. Thus the priest, according to the Liturgy associated with St Basil, prays regarding the bread and wine, "*Show them* to be your Body and your Blood."

To assert this mediating role of bread, wine, oil, and water is somewhat challenging for those who consider these things only to be mute and inactive symbols of what God is doing. From the beginning, though, Christians East and West have taken quite seriously the words of Jesus (*This is my body. . . . this is my blood*, Mt 26.26, 28), St Paul (*We were buried with Him unto death by baptism*, Rom 6.4), St Peter (*Baptism . . . now saves you*, 1 Pet 3.21) and St James, the brother of our Lord (*Anoint with oil . . . and the prayer . . . will raise the sick*

[25]C. S. Lewis, *Mere Christianity* (New York: HarperCollins Paperback, 2001 [1st ed. 1952]), 193, 196.

[26]This term was first used as early as the second century by the martyr Ignatius of Antioch.

*person up . . . and he will be forgiven*, Jas 5.14–15). Not until the time of the Protestant Reformation were these physical objects considered to be simply a focal point or mnemonic aids; rather they were seen as the very locus of God's communion with us. Those who are still in doubt regarding the sacramental nature of these things, when used in worship, may consider the thoughtful words of Fr Alexander Schmemann, whose little book *For the Life of the World* caused a revolution of thought among many Christians. In it he explains the potential sacramental nature of God's entire cosmos, used by the Lord to bring us to Himself, to deepen our understanding, and to even complete what He has begun:

> The term "sacramental" means . . . that the world, as . . . cosmos [and] in . . . history, is an *epiphany* of God, a means of His revelation, presence, and power. . . . The world—in worship—is revealed in its true nature and vocation as a "sacrament." We *need* water and oil, bread and wine in order to be in communion with God and to know Him. . . . We can only worship in time, yet it is worship that ultimately not only reveals the meaning of time, but truly "renews" time itself. There is no worship without the participation of the body, without words and silence, light and darkness, movement and stillness—yet it is in and through worship that all these essential expressions of man . . . are . . . revealed in their highest and deepest meaning.[27]

Fr Schmemann's short but accessible study helps us to understand more deeply C. S. Lewis' insight concerning God's regard for matter and how He uses it for our healing and well-being, to put in us "the God-life."

----

[27]Alexander Schmemann, *For the Life of the World: Sacraments and Orthodoxy*, 3rd ed. (Yonkers: St. Vladimir's Seminary Press, 2018), 142–43.

## Relics, Icons, and the Scriptures

Beyond the debate concerning the sacraments, there are even more fraught questions among Christians concerning the use of icons and relics. Some Christians believe that the use of icons is actually forbidden in the ten commandments (*make no graven image*), and the use of relics is simply superstitious. Let us begin with relics, since there is no seeming prohibition against them: indeed there appear to be scriptural precedents for their use. A relic is an honored object, either part of the holy person's body, or part of his or her clothing or other belongings, which has a beneficial effect upon someone. In the Old Testament, we might think immediately of Elisha's happy reception of Elijah's cloak, and how it becomes the tangible sign of the "double portion" of the older prophet's power, which Elisha inherits, and uses to glorify God. Elisha and this cloak have a long history together: it was by casting his cloak upon the younger man that Elijah made him a disciple (1 Kings/3 Kingdoms 19.19)[28] and Elisha saw his teacher part the waters with this cloak (2 Kings/4 Kingdoms 2.8). So, after the master-prophet has been assumed into heaven, leaving his cloak as a parting gift, we are not surprised to see Elisha use the cloak in a similar way, striking and parting the waters, and calling out, *Where is the* LORD, *the God of Elijah?* (2 Kings/4 Kingdoms 2.14). The answer to his question is evident: the LORD is now with him, as his God, evident in the power of the bequeathed cloak. Evidently, even with Elisha's death, this presence did not depart, since the younger prophet's very bones raised to life a dead man whose body was cast into Elisha's sepulcher (2 Kings/4 Kingdoms 13.20–21).

---

[28]In the Septuagint, 1 and 2 Samuel and 1 and 2 Kings are called 1, 2, 3, and 4 Kingdoms.

Nor are such phenomena confined to the Old Testament, as vivid illustrations of God's presence for a people that had not yet seen the LORD in the flesh. We move again into the Acts of the Apostles, a book that describes the mighty acts of God that Jesus assured His disciples they would perform by the power of the Holy Spirit (Jn 14.12). Most readers note the restoration of sight to Paul, the healing of the lame, and so on, as indications of the continued healing work of Jesus through the apostles' hands, as they are laid upon the sick. But there are also two intriguing, even somewhat bizarre, episodes that involve less proximate healing. Hopeful people put their sick loved ones on the side of the road, in anticipation that the passing shadow of Peter will heal them (Acts 5.15–16); they also lay articles of Paul's clothing on the sick, who are cured (Act 19.12). Those not predisposed to seeing material things imbued with God's power may explain this away as superstition (but Luke does not call it this) or as God's accommodation to human weakness (but nowhere does Luke call us beyond such "infantile" ideas, though he has plenty to say, by means of the narrative, about the evils of magic). No, it is simply assumed that physical phenomena like shadows cast by Peter, or personal effects of Paul, can have a healing power, like magnetism in a chain of needles, as it were. The material world is seen as a natural location for God's energies, because God has entered deeply into our world in the Incarnation, and now has come to dwell with the disciples of the incarnate one.

The healing grace that is not impeded by geographical distance comes to be understood, as in the case with Elijah and Elisha, as available to those at a temporal distance from the wonder-worker. For example, second-century Christians believed that the bones of Polycarp—a disciple of the apostle John—had similar power to that of Elisha, since they rescued these bones after his martyrdom, as though they were more precious than jewels, and installed them in

an honored resting place where Christians would gather to pray.[29]
In the Church's ongoing experience of grace that continues to reside
with us through the martyrs and saints, it seemed natural for cathe-
drals and other churches to be founded as places to enshrine the
bodily remnants of their patron saints, or other beloved departed.
Sheltered within the altars of these places of worship were the clothing and bones of holy ones, as well as parts of Christ's holy cross. In
the Orthodox Tradition, a relic is also sewn into the *antimension* (or
*antimins*)—a cloth that serves "instead of the table" (a literal translation), so that Eucharist can be celebrated in places other than the
actual church. Interestingly, in the Ethiopian tradition, the relics are
kept in a wooden tablet that is given the name "Ark of the Covenant."
These practices existed in the early Church, but were rendered normative, both for East and West, in the Second Ecumenical Council
of Nicaea (787), which not only vindicated the practice of making and
venerating icons, but also decreed that every altar should contain a
relic. In all this, we are reminded of the Old Testament ark, which
housed the manna, the budding staff of Aaron, and the tablets of the
Law. Moreover, we may call to mind the vision of the Apocalypse,
where the saints pray *beneath the altar*. Kept in this way at the focal
point of worship, the altar, relics were meant to strengthen those who
worshipped, just as the prayers of these saints did the same. Along
with the verbal reminders in the Liturgy concerning those who had

[29] *Martyrdom of Polycarp* 18. In the words of eyewitnesses to his martyrdom: "Thus we, at last, took up his bones, more precious than precious stones,
and finer than gold, and put them where it was meet. There the Lord will
permit us to come together according to our power in gladness and joy, and
celebrate the birthday of his martyrdom, both in memory of those who have
already contested, and for the practice and training of those whose fate it shall
be" (ibid., 18.2–3; Kirsopp Lake trans.).

departed to be with the LORD, those who gathered for worship did so in places where their older, deceased brothers and sisters in the faith were bodily present in the relics. In this way, the whole Church, living and "asleep," became physically proximate to each other, as the LORD was also present with them in the reading of the Gospel, and in the consecrated Bread and Wine.

The same council that commended relics to the Church also ratified the use of icons, which were being contested by "iconoclasts," who had a less physical understanding of the faith. This topic is more complex, both theologically and hermeneutically, than that of relics. To understand why the historic Church, both East and West, defended the use of icons, we must think both about the implications of the Incarnation (as the Church Fathers of that time did), and about the distinction between the eras of the Old and New Testaments. Certainly, there is a clear precept against making images of God, which some have interpreted as a prohibition against any image-making:

> You shall not make for yourself a graven image, or any likeness of anything that is in heaven above, or that is in the earth beneath, or that is in the water under the earth; you shall not bow down to them or serve them; for I the LORD your God am a jealous God, visiting the iniquity of the fathers upon the children to the third and the fourth generation of those who hate me, but showing steadfast love to thousands of those who love me and keep my commandments. (Exodus 20.4–6, RSV)

A literal reading of the first part of the command, taken in isolation from the next few phrases, may take this as absolute prohibition against the visual arts. Of course, we know that this cannot be the case, since the same LORD goes on to command Moses and allow Solomon to make images of the cherubim (Ex 25.20), almonds and flowers (Ex 25.33), pomegranates (Ex 28.34), palm trees (1 Kings/3Kingdoms 6.32), and even of animals (1 Kings/3 Kingdoms 7.25), and to place these within the tabernacle or the temple. Obviously, the prohibition is against the production of images *for the purpose of worshipping them,* that is, to prevent idolatry, or the worship of the created realities that these images represent: *You shall not bow down to them or serve them.*

The prohibition against making images is not absolute, then, as most Christians have acknowledged through the centuries, readily acknowledging that the faithful can be visual artists, just as they can be musicians, to the glory of God. Indeed, representative and symbolic art is often used in a mediating capacity, as an extension of the artist's desire to help others, not only when the theme is explicitly biblical or theological, but whenever he or she moves others to see the beauty of creation. In this ministry, icons take on a particular role, one that was championed by the likes of St John of Damascus during the iconoclastic controversy, and that was settled for the Church in the Second Council of Nicaea (AD 787) of the undivided Church. Historically, most Christians had readily accepted artistic endeavors in general, but there still remained the question about picturing God Himself, and whether that inevitably leads to idolatry. A further complication that arose in the seventh century was the rise of Islam, which cherishes some traditions (though no clear Qu'ranic verses) that prohibit picturing God, Mohammed, and even living things. The doctrine of the Incarnation, rejected by Muslims, featured strongly in the Christian defense of icons at this time. Indeed, the argument that St John of Damascus made, adopted by the council, depends foundationally upon the revolutionary change in our reality when God became a human, indeed, *the* Human Being *par excellence*: though "the invisible things of God" "are made visible" dimly, even in creation (cf. Rom 1.19–20), the Incarnation has shown forth God's nature in an incontrovertible manner. If God has made what was mysterious visible, then we are at liberty to depict it; indeed, it is completely appropriate and faithful to show this revelation visibly. To paint an icon of Christ is the pictorial equivalent of proclaiming the gospel, that God became Man for our sake.[30]

St John, indeed, begins his treatise not in terms of proclaiming the freedom of Christians to engage in the making of icons, but by speaking about the "danger" that he perceives in the arguments of the "iconoclasts." These icon-smashers are, in effect, ripping the seamless robe of Christ, and cutting His body into pieces by questioning the Gospel and Holy Tradition. Just as we have seen in our interpretation of the command in Exodus, St John says that it is given to prevent idolatry, not to proscribe the veneration of holy images. But, he says, Christians are no longer infants, prone to such idolatry, and are not tempted to confine the mysterious God in a single place, as with those who adore idols. Instead, we have the mind of Christ, knowing that the omnipresent God became human, visible to our eyes—and so we can depict this. As we now know Christ, we will not be tempted to confuse worship of God with veneration of other things: worship is one thing, veneration another. Even in the Old Testament, he points out, there are degrees of veneration, and some human beings are treated with great respect. Clearly, even the Old Testament shows exceptions to the rule against the making of images, and we must accept that *there is a time for everything* (Eccl 3.1). The time for rejecting images of God has now passed, since God Himself has come in

[30]It should be pointed out that, in the Eastern Tradition, icons are not simply religious art, but are painted according to canons that prevent over-sentimentalization or objectification of the image. Some music is not helpful for worship, though it may have other uses; some representations are, in a similar way, not considered appropriate for that context. Typically Orthodox do not, for example, use statues in worship, as is the habit elsewhere. Anything that prevents the worshipper from passing *through* the icon to the actual one represented, and thus to God, is avoided.

the flesh, among us, hallowing the material world. Further, because human beings bear the image of Christ, we should especially honor those who have been faithful unto death. This may be done in icons that show their holiness:

> The first is as a form of worship, which we offer to God, alone by nature worthy of veneration. Then there is the veneration offered, on account of God who is naturally venerated, to his friends and servants.[31]
>
> The saints during their earthly lives were filled with the Holy Spirit, and when they fulfill their course, the grace of the Holy Spirit does not depart from their souls or their bodies in the tombs, or from their likenesses and holy images, not by the nature of these things, but by grace and power.[32]

As we can see from St John Damascene's treatment of this subject (and these principles were enshrined in the Second Council of Nicaea) it is not simply a matter of defending the use of icons, whether of Christ or the saints. Rather, it is a matter of understanding how God uses matter for our sanctification, of acknowledging the real communion of saints, and of honoring the mediating power of our holy forebears, male and female, who bear the image of Christ. He makes a distinction in the kind of reverence offered to Christ, who is God, and the saints, who have the image of God imprinted upon them by grace. Yet both, he says, are honored, according to their due, by the way that we attend to icons. In a statement that has become famous, he clarifies: "I depict what I have seen of God. I do not venerate matter, I venerate the fashioner of matter, who became matter for my sake and accepted to dwell in matter and through matter worked my salvation,

---

[31]Damascene, *On the Divine Images* 1.14 (PPS 24:27).
[32]Damascene, *On the Divine Images* 1.19.

and I will not cease from reverencing matter, through which my salvation was worked. I do not reverence it as God—far from it."[33]

Indeed, our celebration of the saints in this way leads to a more robust and joyful worship, says St John, and is consonant with our love for the Church, since the saints are "her trophies," showing what God has done in our midst.[34] Throughout his argument, the Damascene argues both from Scripture and from Holy Tradition, reminding his readers that there are many customs kept alive by word of mouth (three immersions in Baptism, worship towards the east, and the words surrounding Communion), and that St Paul himself commended cleaving to apostolic Tradition (2 Thess 2.15).[35] The gift of icons, then, verifies the saving and sanctifying work of God, and forms a natural and ancient part of our life together as the Body of Christ. When we honor them, we honor those whom they depict, and so we worship the God who has perfected them. Moreover, if we listen to those who have a deeper experience with icons, we may be surprised to hear of healing and wisdom that comes through them. Not a few worshippers, including even visitors who were not Christians prior to their encounter, have been transformed by the ongoing power evident in some icons that, for example, inexplicably and copiously stream myrrh. These become, for some seekers, like the perfume lavishly poured on Jesus' feet, relieving illness, and preparing those who receive the blessing for everything that is to come their way. In this way, icons become an essential vehicle for the mediating love of brothers and sisters who are now with the LORD. Together

[33]Damascene, *On the Divine Images* 1.16 (PPS 24:29).

[34]Damascene, *On the Divine Images* 1.23–26.

[35]Damascene, *On the Divine Images* 1.28. The Damascene acknowledges the source of these examples (triune immersion, worship facing east, and the prayers of the Eucharist): St Basil the Great's *On the Holy Spirit*, where he describes *agrapha dogmata* (unwritten teachings).

with them, we are all called to have formed in us the *new Adam*, whom Christ Himself embodies fully (Gal 4.19).

## But Is This Magic?

Unexpected things, then, have been reported in Scriptures, in Tradition, and in the present day, regarding the ongoing power of those saints who are with the LORD, made effective through asking their intercessions, through their representation in icons, and through their holy remains. What are we to make of such reports? And if these things are not sheer imagination, how are we to see these as different from magic? Indeed, some earnest Christians have charged that to pray for the help of a deceased saint is nothing other than a Christianized form of necromancy—magic performed by means of the dead. Some outside of the Church have likewise scoffed at confidence in any miracles, considering them the Christian equivalent to a gullible acceptance of magic, a throwback to the time before science was properly practiced. Others outside the Church, in our postmodern age, have abandoned the dominant view of the modern period that miracles are impossible because they break the laws that scientists regularly observe in nature. Indeed, I remember, about twenty-five years ago, the first time that I got a new response, when I quoted—as I habitually did in my introduction class to the New Testament—a well-known dictum of the (in)famous scholar Rudolf Bultmann, that it is impossible to avail oneself of modern medicine and to use light-bulbs while continuing to believe in the spirit-world of the New Testament.[36] For the first time, the statement was not

---

[36]Rudolph Bultmann, *The New Testament and Mythology and Other Basic Writings*, trans. and ed. Schubert M. Ogden (Philadelphia, PA: Fortress, 1984), 14.

met with nods, but with puzzled and blank stares. It occurred to me that many of my students had finally moved out of the modernist paradigm, and no longer had a dispositional allergy to the possibility of signs and wonders in the New Testament. When I asked one of them to explain, he opined that there are many strange things in the world, so why not in the early history of Christianity? For this new generation, the problem was now the particular claims of Jesus and His followers, not the flouting of the materialist disposition of scientism. Our day is complex, then, as we try to distinguish—for a mixed audience—between magic, the unknown potential of creation, or the power of the human spirit in itself, on the one hand, and the Christian testimony to God using material means in unusual ways for the benefit of human beings and all creation. What is it about divine signs associated with saints that has commended itself to the Church as an appropriate expression of who God is, and who we are? How are these things different from the ancient view of magic, or a more variegated contemporary openness to mystical events, coupled with the untapped but latent power of human beings?

It may be helpful to return yet again to the composite book Luke-Acts as we probe these questions. There we see that, from the beginning, the Church has sharply distinguished between magic and miracle. (The cynical may say that the only real difference is that miracles are supposed to be performed by Christians, not magicians. But we will see more significant differences than apparent agency.) Let us consider first Luke 10.1–21, in which the LORD commissions the Seventy to present the good news to towns in Galilee, equipped with power from on high. When they return, they are delighted at their power and success, and Jesus redirects them to what is more significant—they should rejoice to be included in God's family, and give glory to God. Jesus tells them that there has been a cosmic shift so that the Enemy no longer holds the world in slavery, and this victory should also command their attention, as they worship the God who has brought new life to the world. Not power, but humility, is the hallmark of this God who is among them. All the miracles of healing, feeding, turning of water to wine, and even the destruction of the fig tree are not mere pyrotechnics of a powerfully "showy" God, but for the benefit of those whom He loves beyond measure. They will soon enough see that God's greatest glory is the cross.

As we move further into Luke's story, we revisit the strange story of St Paul, and the miracles done by his clothing, brought to the sick (Acts 19.11–12). How is this different from, say, a white-magic horcrux in the world of Harry Potter, where an object holds within it a vestige of power from a particular person? The narrative of Acts itself makes it clear that we are not to understand these events in a mechanistic way, as though the articles possess power in and of themselves. Rather, they are connected with the apostle, who himself is intimately connected with the LORD. Already before this story of St Paul's healing clothing, the narrative warned us against magic through the tale of Simon (Acts 8.5–24, considered in this present book in chapter two). Again, several chapters after the healing by St Paul, the seven sons of Sceva fancy themselves able to use magical incantations including the name of Jesus and His servant Paul, in order to demonstrate power like Paul's (Acts 19). But the response of the demons shows that this concept is mistaken—*We have heard of Paul and Jesus, but who are YOU?* (Acts 19.15). The demons recognize no real connection between these would-be magicians and either Jesus or Paul! It is neither a magical object nor name that heals, but the Holy One Himself, who deigns to delegate authority to His apostles. As one who is incarnate among those who are flesh-and-blood, He uses embodied human beings, and even their clothing, to care for His people in a material world. The LORD who gave Baptism and the Eucharist continues to work in the material world, not to give a display of raw power or magic, but to show His love. The signs are an extension of His compassion and humility, as the greatest one comes into our world to rescue the least. And so it is that the apostles have seen *the light of the knowledge of the glory of God* in Jesus (2 Cor 4.6), and they demonstrate that radiance in their own earthen vessels (2 Cor 4.1–7); and so it is that all of us, in turn, will reflect that same glory (2 Cor 3.18).

It is, after all, not only miracles, prayers to the saints, or the use of physical objects in worship that can tend towards magical thinking. So, too, can prayer in general, when we adopt a stance of "positive thinking," "name it and claim it," or presumption that we always know God's will. Our prayers must be directed towards the LORD in humility, seeking wisdom and His favor. Any attempt to manipulate God, any misconception that the power resides in us, and not in Him, any forgetting that He knows our needs before we ask, puts us on the brink of such magical thinking. How astonishing it is that God has called us into His council, and invites us to participate, together with Him, in the reclaiming of the world! When we ask others to join us in our requests—whether those whom we see around us, or those who have gone before into His presence—God is not swayed by the sheer number of petitioners, nor by their status. Prayers together should not be seen as the equivalent of a political "petition" that changes the mind of the one in control! Rather, it is our joy to work together within His will, knowing that He hears where two or three are gathered together, and where we join our hearts with the holy ones who are anything but dead in His presence. God's use of physical objects such as icons or relics (the elements "below" us in the world), or His commissioning of angelic beings (those "above" us in the cosmos) may seem unusual in our post-Enlightenment experience, but it is not out of the divine character. For He is the LORD of all, and has declared His intention to reconcile things in heaven and things on the earth (Col 1.20), beginning with the wood of the cross.

In all this we have seen how mediation is something that especially characterizes the Church, but also that God mediates to us in startling ways, by using objects connected with the saints, and by using beings whom we do not normally see, who nevertheless remain interconnected with our human world, awaiting the resurrection and the new creation. This interconnection in itself holds some surprises. It seems to be the normative view of Scripture that there is a kind of hierarchical order from God, through the angels, through human beings, through the animals, on through to the inanimate creation. If something goes wrong in the upper levels, the bottom is affected, and if something happens above that is good, it will likewise make its impact below. So as St Paul puts it, the creation was subjected to a futile life of death not by its own fault, but by the Fall of our first parents, so that at the present time the entire creation looks to the future human restoration as the time of its own release from death (Rom 8.18–23). On this principle, we would naturally think of mediation from the top down, with the more powerful helping the weaker—and so this is modelled in our own salvation as the Strong Man, Jesus, has bound our demonic enemy (Mk 3.27). And yet, as we have already seen in the song of the Virgin Mary's Magnificat, the whole story of our salvation involves reversals, for the Greatest has become the Least for our sake. In echo, the weak now are given the means to confound the strong, and the foolishness of God undoes the wisdom of man. Human beings instruct angels in the mystery of the ages; material objects mediate God's grace to human beings. Out of the mouth of infants God ordains praise! There is, indeed, an orderly mediation by which we can expect aid from those who are stronger than we are. But there is a mutual mediation as well, in which the weaker, paradoxically, witnesses to the stronger. In seeing this joining together of those things we thought divided, we come to celebrate something far more dynamic and surprising than a bland, pantheistic "circle of life." Instead, we may rejoice that both ordered and mutual mediation are being used by the LORD until the joyful time comes when God will be all in all (1 Cor 15.28; cf. Eph 1.23).

CHAPTER 4

# Mothers, Mediation, and Our Mediatrix

We have seen that mediation is expressed both in terms of reciprocity among members of the family of God—in fact, among members of God's entire creation—and also in terms of a natural "order," where the stronger help the weaker. The presence of mutual mediation means that those who expect a completely ordered or hierarchical process of teaching, intercession, and other forms of aid will be stunned from time to time. As the Mother of our Lord puts it, *He has shown strength with his arm; He has scattered the proud in the imagination of their hearts; He has put down the mighty from their thrones, and exalted those who are lowly* (Lk 1.51–52). Though the LORD mightily used the educated rabbi Saul (in the Gentile Church, St Paul), Jesus' first-called apostles were uneducated fishermen, who upset the intelligentsia of the time with their ability to speak boldly on behalf of God: *When they saw the courage of Peter and John, and noted that they were uneducated ordinary men, they were astonished and they realized that these men had been with Jesus* (Acts 4.13) . As an Orthodox hymn for Pentecost puts it,

> Blessed art Thou, O Christ our God,
> who hast revealed the fishermen as most wise
> by sending down upon them the Holy Spirit:

through them Thou didst draw the world into Thy net.

O Lover of Man, Glory to Thee!

By his new identity in the Church, the formally trained Paul learns to consider himself *least among the apostles* because of his persecution of the Church, and reminds the sophisticated Corinthians of God's ability to use those considered *foolish* or *weak* (1 Cor 1.20–31). In that same letter, he encourages Christian women who are married to pagans, asking them rhetorically, *Wife, how do you know whether you will save your husband?* (1 Cor 7.16). Though he goes on to reverse the question and address the men, his starting point is the possible influence of those whom many considered the *weaker vessel* (cf. 1 Pet 3.7). No doubt this was a common occurrence in the early Church, as women seemed to more readily accept the gospel than Greek or Roman men, for whom humility would not have been understood as a virtue. We should not, then, be surprised to discover that the Christian story is replete with women who mediate even on behalf of those who possessed more power than they—beginning with the "blessed" role of a young girl from an obscure town in Galilee, rather than a high-born male from Jerusalem. In this chapter, while recognizing that mediation is a calling of *all* those who are in the Body of Christ, as we each learn to express God's generosity and love to others, we will look to what seems to be a special "charism" of mediation for women, and then go on to probe the very particular role of the Virgin Mary, who bore the incarnate God for our sake.

## Matthew, Matriarchs, Mothers, and Mediation

Those who know something about the New Testament might think that, for the purposes of discovering ministering women in the Gospels, the Fourth Gospel, with the prominence of Jesus' Mother, the Samaritan woman, and Mary Magdalene, would be most promising. Or they might be aware of Luke's special interest in women and his particular selection of parables that include them (e.g., the lost coin, Lk 15.8–10). It is Matthew's Gospel, however, that begins with the surprising notice of matriarchs in Jesus' ancestry—surprising, at least, so far as contemporary critical scholars are concerned, since they might expect this more Jewish Gospel to display a decidedly patriarchal worldview. Further, since we are here concerned with the relationship between mediation and the character of the Church, some might not think the first Gospel to be very promising. After all, unlike Luke-Acts, which has large portions dedicated directly to the Church, Matthew's ecclesiology remains only implicit. However, the well-developed instruction in the Sermon on the Mount, Jesus' words to Peter about building His Church, the provocative parabolic questions about the identity of God's people, and the brief descriptions of the community around Jesus—both apostles and attendant women—all indicate that the nature of the Church is a significant, though muted, theme in this Gospel. Commenting upon the communal aspect of Peter's confession in Matthew's Gospel, Origen, for example, gives this encouragement: "If we, too, say to ourselves, 'You are the Christ, the Son of the living God,' then we also become Peter."[1]

One contemporary expert in this Gospel explains how the doctrine of the Church is seen in Matthew's particular understanding of New Covenant righteousness, in which the Christian "family" becomes operative:

Matthew alone among the synoptics specifies the "disciples" in the following statement: "And stretching out his hand towards his disciples, he said, 'Here are my mothers and brothers! For

---

[1] Origen, *Commentaria in Evangelium secundum Matthaeum* (PG 13:997, my trans.).

whoever does the will of my Father in heaven is my brother,
and sister, and mother'" (12.49–50). The members of the new
community, the *ekklēsia*, constitute a new family that does the
will of the Father, i.e., that lives righteously. This family has an
enabling role; its members provide a significant resource for the
achievement of righteousness. . . . [I]t is the larger church that
finally holds the individual accountable.[2]

This scholar does not go deeply into the role of women in the Church,
as it emerges in this Gospel. But he does exhibit how Matthew can
be an excellent source for our query into a specific characteristic of
ecclesiology—mutual mediation—within the Christian Tradition.

Before beginning, it is imperative to realize that our concern
for the position of women is a contemporary one. Though Church
Fathers touch upon this issue (e.g., St John Chrysostom in his ful-
some words concerning St Photini as more faithful than her male
counterparts[3]), most of them concentrate upon the major burden of
Matthew's Gospel, that is, the person of the Christ. Moreover, there
is a particular "flavor" to the discussion of present-day New Testament scholars concerning the status of women that we cannot ignore
in focusing upon what we must admit to be a secondary issue in the
Gospel. In this particular section, then, we will listen and adjudicate
between today's scholars more than in the rest of this study, though
we will also hear what the Fathers have to say. Keeping in mind that
our assessment of this aspect may be somewhat exaggerated because
of our context, we will show the surprising prominence of women as

[2]Donald A. Hagner, "Holiness and Ecclesiology: The Church in Matthew," Kent E. Brower and Andy Johnson, eds, *Holiness and Ecclesiology in the
New Testament* (Grand Rapids, MI: Eerdmans, 2007), 52.

[3]Chrysostom, *Homilies on the Gospel according to John* 34.1 (NPNF[1] 14:118).

mediators in Matthew, considering them as a group before moving on to the Virgin Mary.

One of the first things the astute reader notices in opening Matthew's Gospel is that he begins by marking the key women in the ancestry of Jesus. As we move further into the Gospel, we see how women, both named and unnamed, take on intriguing and varied helping roles: Rahab in the genealogy, Peter's mother-in-law who is healed in order to serve, the Canaanite woman who makes an appeal for her daughter, the patronesses of Jesus in His ministry and at the cross, Pilate's wife who tries to avert evil, and the women disciples' joyful announcement to the apostles. All these provide a pattern of mediation that might be intentionally traced by the evangelist, though authorial motive is notoriously difficult to pin down. Among these positive figures, there are also skewed representations of female mediation in the vignettes peopled by Salome and Herodias, and the mother of James and John—though her intervention is merely human, and not vicious. An entire book could be written on the helping function of women in Matthew, but for our purposes we will explore Rahab, the Canaanite mother, and the women disciples who encounter the Christ as they speed on their way in obedience to the angelic command to proclaim the Resurrection. Each of these will be seen as mediators whose actions benefit not simply those whom they meet in their specific narratives, but the people of God as a whole.

## Rahab: Mediating through Matriarchy

Rahab is, like the other three women in the Matthean genealogy (Tamar, the wife of Uriah, and Ruth), an unlikely figure to put forward as a model. Already in the Hebrew tradition, though, she stands as a righteous Gentile, because of her faith-in-action on behalf of the Hebrew spies. She would have been considered heroic in the same mode as a Dutch resistance family that hid Jews from Nazi aggression. Yet her significance is far greater: she not only stands between the endangered Hebrew spies and the leaders of the Canaanite city of Jericho, but also between the Hebrew warriors and her own family, which is gathered safely under her roof, marked by scarlet, in an echo of the Passover blood (Josh 2.18). On top of this, once the conquest is over, she comes out from the conquered city, and joins herself and her family to Israel, living in humility outside the camp. We might suspect that it is not only her Canaanite identity but also her previous profession as a prostitute that lead to this exigency: the spies owe her gratitude, but the purity of the camp is also at issue.

At this point we might think that the story puts the Hebrews in a mediating position *for her*, but her union with them (incomplete though this co-dwelling was) is amplified in Jewish tradition, which speaks of her marriage to none other than Joshua,[4] and which was said to produce the famous figures such as Hilkiah, Baruch, Ezekiel, and Hulda. Her worthiness to be a progenitor of this royal line is picturesquely portrayed in a midrash (a narrative expansion of the biblical story) where she appears before the Almighty, entreating, "By the merit of three things pardon me: the rope, the window, and the wall."[5] It would seem that in Jewish tradition her righteousness is founded upon her actions and her cleaving to Israel, with all

---

[4]Richard Bauckham cites the Jewish writing *b. Meg. 14b-15a* in "Tamar's Ancestry and Rahab's Marriage: Two Problems in the Matthean Genealogy," *Novum Testamentum* (1995): 324.

[5]Cited from *Mekhilta de-Rabbi Ishmael, Masekhta de-Amalek, Yitro* by Tamar Kadari, "Rahab: Midrash and Aggadah," in *Shalvi/Hyman Encyclopedia of Jewish Women* (31 December 1999), Jewish Women's Archive. <https://jwa.org/encyclopedia/article/rahab-midrash-and-aggadah>.

that follows being seen as embellishments upon her critical role in the Conquest.

Christian tradition also bears in mind her cunning and courage, but shapes this in a different way. Matthew's genealogy, following a different line than other Jewish traditions, speaks of her as the wife of Salmon, by whom she conceived Boaz.[6] Boaz would himself, of course, take a mediating position for Ruth: like mother, like son. With deftness, the evangelist reminds us of the strange presence of this Gentile in the history of David, and how David was himself indebted both to Jewish fathers and Gentile mothers. Though any reader of Matthew cognizant of the book of Joshua would know that Rahab sinned in her body, he or she would be directed to meditate instead upon what she *became* in her body—an ancestor of the Messiah. Her very matriarchy is a mediating role that benefits the household of God, just as her canny actions stood in the breach both for those whom she hid and helped to escape, and for her family. Rahab is named, remembered, and is seen as valuable in her own person for salvation history.

We should note that Rahab is celebrated elsewhere in the New Testament as an example of faith-in-action (Jas 2.25), and in a surprising move as part of Hebrew's celebrated roll-call of faith. In the sequence, Rahab appears after Moses, where we would expect to find Joshua, and she is pictured not only as faithful, but as one who receives others *with peace*, as the LORD Himself does (Heb 11.31). With subtlety, the writer further aligns her with Jesus, who also went *outside the camp* and so blessed God's people—indeed, He and she are patterns for the faithful, who are also called to suffer outside the

---

[6]For an interesting theory of Matthew's sources, see Richard Bauckham, "Tamar's Ancestry."

camp (Heb 13.11–13). In the next generation of Christians, *1 Clement* celebrates her for her hospitality, her faith, and also for her prophetic words and actions: not only does she predict the success of the Hebrews, but prefigures by the scarlet cord that *through the blood of the Lord there shall be redemption unto all . . . [who] believe and hope on God.*[7] We cannot know how many of these associations concerning Rahab were common currency in the earliest Christian proclamation, and would have been implied by Matthew's placement of her in the first part of his Gospel. What we can say is that for the early Christian community, Rahab was notable for her non-Jewish pedigree, her nonconformist hospitality, her effective faith in the God of Israel, her adherence to the community (however humble), and her presence among Jesus' forebears. In Matthew, by her placement among the ancestors of the Messiah, she is rendered a notable mediatrix not only for her immediate family and the spies but for all who are part of the New Covenant.

Speaking of the four women in the genealogy as a whole, Stanley Hauerwas remarks, "These women are not clearly from the people of Israel, yet they serve God's providential care of Israel by quite literally making the Davidic line possible . . . [T]hese women use their wits to force the men of Israel to claim them as members of God's promise. They prefigure the Canaanite woman."[8] I would comment that this prefiguring function is particularly true of Rahab, who was herself a Canaanite, and displayed the same uncommon faith as this marginalized and unnamed woman who came to Jesus. We shall go on to see that the Matthean passage involving this Gentile mother,

[7] *1 Clement* 12.7 (Lightfoot trans.).

[8] Stanley Hauerwas, *Brazos Theological Commentary on Matthew* (Grand Rapids, MI: Brazos, 2015 [1st ed. 2006]), 33.

and her care for her child, reiterates several of the themes associated with Rahab in early Christian proclamation.

## *The Canaanite: Stand-in for Daughter, the Gentiles, and the Needy*

Like Rahab, the unnamed Canaanite woman is a figure of faith. This is emphasized in Matthew's Gospel, over that of Mark, which does not include Jesus' concluding words: *O woman, great is your faith!* (Mt 15.28). This is not an exclamation that celebrates the woman's earnestness and persistence, however, but the means by which Jesus puts forward the woman's faith as a pattern. The woman's faith is "great" because it is directed towards a great God, the only true God. Indeed, the contours of her faith are sketched in the very first actions and words of the unnamed woman. Like Rahab of old, who acknowledged the true God of heaven and earth, this Canaanite comes out from her village and calls for mercy from *the Son of David* (15.22). In using this name, she reiterates what Matthew has said regarding Jesus from the first verse of his Gospel, in consonance with the genealogy itself: *David the king begot Solomon . . . and Jacob begot Joseph, the husband of Mary, of whom was born Jesus, who is called the Christ* (1.6, 16). The shape of her faith is, like that of Rahab, both aggressive and canny, and it is expressed on behalf of someone other than herself. A comparison of the tone of the exchange between the spies and Rahab, and Jesus and the woman, discloses many similarities: both are bold to ask, and confident that their benefactor can deliver.

One difference, of course, is that, unlike the Hebrew spies, Jesus appears unwilling to comply. But we must remember that Rahab had already demonstrated her sincerity through her self-endangering action, whereas this Gentile woman encountering Jesus must be "tested" as a prospective proselyte. Charles H. Talbert, a New

Testament scholar, points to the repeated requests of the woman, and reminds us that in Jewish practice a proselyte was only admitted after four requests.[9] It is interesting, too, that her interchange with Jesus includes the theme of hospitality—who can be admitted to the table—with the woman humbly not claiming her rights, but nevertheless gesturing towards the overflowing generosity of God, who is so bountiful that His nourishment overflows any expected bounds. St Augustine sees this open-heartedness as a picture of those humble Gentiles who are grafted into the Church (cf. Rom 11.17–23), commenting, "See . . . how in this woman who was a Canaanite—who came from the Gentiles and represented a type (namely, a figure of the Church)—how her humility is highly praised."[10]

Her adoring "worship" of Jesus (Greek, *proskyneō;* Mt 15.25) is aptly followed by her confession of unworthy confidence in the LORD of life. Rather than being scandalized by the prospect of a prostrate woman who has accepted the role of a dog for the sake of her child, generations before our own commended this extravagant behavior to worshippers in general, whether male or female. Indeed, her humility and confidence in the divine Giver has been embraced in Western worship. Hauerwas notes that this woman has taught generations of Christians how to speak: "We are not worthy so much as to gather up the crumbs under thy Table. But thou art the same Lord whose property is always to have mercy."[11] As Rahab was content outside the camp, so the Canaanite is content with crumbs—but both will

[9]Charles H. Talbert, *Matthew,* Paidea Commentary Series (Grand Rapids: Eerdmans, 2010), 190. In noting this tradition, he cites *Ruth Rabbah* 2.16.

[10]Augustine, *Sermon* 27.11 (PL 38:487; NPNF[1] 6:345).

[11]Hauerwas, *Matthew,* 32. Hauerwas, like many others, connects the woman's argument regarding crumbs under the table with these traditional words of "humble access" to the Eucharist, as used in the Anglican communion, as well as in St Tikhon's Orthodox western rite.

be joined to the household in far more significant ways. Rahab as matriarch, and this unnamed pagan mother as an exemplar of persistent and humble faith, show those who follow what it is to trust an unknown God to the point of bargaining, humbly asking for help, worshipping, and receiving divine hospitality. In their words and actions, they mediate a lively pattern to many others to follow. The Canaanite, too, becomes a "forerunner of our faith,"[12] instructing us in posture and in words how the living God is to be approached.

## *The Two Marys: Teaching Worship and Proclaiming the Gospel*

Two other women, both named Mary, also teach us a posture of worship, and the importance of mediating words. Luke, as we noted, is usually given pride of place as recording more about the ministering women who accompany Jesus and the twelve throughout their travels. Unlike the shorter ending of Mark, where the women are simply afraid of the angel's Resurrection announcement, Luke *does* have the women go immediately and proclaim the good news to the disciples, who doubt what they say. But Matthew goes even further, including telling details and an extra vignette not found elsewhere. First, the women literally *stand* in stark contrast to the hefty guards at the tomb, who have become as *dead men* at the pyrotechnics of Pascha (Mt 28.4–5). As St John Chrysostom says, "[The angel] addresses [the women] personally: 'I know that *you* seek Jesus who was crucified' . . . In this way he treated them with great honor. It is not for *you* to be afraid, but for those that crucified Jesus."[13] What St John is noticing is that the pronoun "you" is emphasized in the Greek, and that the encouragement

---

[12]Hauerwas, *Matthew*, 48.

[13]Chrysostom, *Homilies on the Gospel according to Matthew* 89.2 (PG 58:784; NPNF[1] 10:527).

*Don't **you** be afraid!* (Mt 28.5) contrasts them with the understandably terrified guards. Indeed, the believing women need not be afraid, for in following Jesus they have been well prepared to see wonders. Matthew also includes two verifying details, each found separately in Mark and Luke, thus richly dignifying the women with rational abilities: they are both to remember what Jesus has said, and to inspect the empty tomb for themselves. Then they are given a detailed message for the disciples, and the angel concludes, *Behold, I have said this **to you!***

Matthew's telling of the story makes it clear that these mediating women are not simply conduits. The interchange that they have with the angel is bookended by direct reference to them: he begins by telling them "*You* need not fear" and caps the interview with "I've told this to *you!*" After all, they have been preparing for this moment for a very long time, including watching the Crucifixion, observing the burial of Jesus in the tomb, and arising early on the Sabbath in order to examine the burial place and make sure everything is in order. As one scholar reminds us, care for the dead (*kēdemonia*) "[i]n the Jewish context . . . surpasses almsgiving, extending hospitality, or visiting the sick."[14]

Matthew seems intent on showing how fitting it is that these women are the first to hear, and soon even to see the truth of things. As R. T. France reminds us, earlier references in Matthew to the Marys have "prepared the ground for the women's role as guarantors of the reality of the resurrection."[15] What France sees as an emphasis on the legitimacy of their report may equally be seen as an honor being given to them. One well-known Orthodox hymn, repeated in a cycle throughout the liturgical year, speaks of this moment with

[14]Talbert, *Matthew*, 286. He uses as evidence for this ideal *t. Pe'ah* 4.9 and *b Sukkah* 49b. We have already shown how care for the dead remains a valued form of piety in the early Christian community.

[15]R. T. France, *The Gospel of Matthew* (Grand Rapids, MI: Eerdmans, 2007), 1098.

exuberance: "When the women disciples heard from the angel the joyful news, they cast away the ancestral curse, and elatedly told the apostles, 'Death is overcome! Christ God has risen, granting the world great mercy!'"[16] Some have argued that they are not even dignified with the name "disciples" in Matthew's Gospel—but we have seen already that Jesus seems to indicate a larger group than the twelve when He gestures to "disciples," calling them His *mother, and brother, and sister* (Mt 12.50). Here He is responding to those who have said that His Mother and brothers have arrived, in search of Him (Mt 12.46). Why would the Lord add "sister" to the list, unless He means to call some of the women present "disciples" as well? Yet the role that these women have is far greater than merely being learners, disciples—they are "apostles to the apostles," mediating their direct knowledge in a way that reverses the curse of the first parents. As Hauerwas remarks, "They leave the tomb in awe, knowing that they are now participants in the kingdom of God."[17]

Their obedient mediation is rewarded in an unexpected manner. Here, alone in the synoptics, the women, as they go on their way, are met by Christ (Mt 28.8–10). As readers, we are accosted with a second of Matthew's dramatic commands, *Behold!* (Greek, *Idou*), matching the repeated use of the term in early chapters (e.g., 1.20, 1.23, 2.19), where readers were told to mark various revelations. It is as though Matthew wants to say, "Behold, the angel has spoken," and now, "Behold, here is something even more wonderful: the LORD Himself." As obedient and God-commissioned mediators, the women are in an appropriate attitude of "fear and great joy." Unlike the duo on the road to Emmaus, their eyes are thus not clouded, nor are they overtaken by Jesus' sudden appearance. His address to them, in the

[16]Troparion of the Resurrection, Tone 4.
[17]Hauerwas, *Matthew*, 245.

Greek, *Chairete,* is simple, if taken colloquially: "Greetings!" But it may be heard sounding even more profound notes, for the word also means "Rejoice!" Their response is by no means casual. They did *not* bow before the angel. But now they come to Jesus, seize His feet, and prostrate themselves *(proskyneō,* yet again). In this posture, they hear again the message, except from Jesus' own mouth: "Do not fear, but tell my brothers where to find me!"

Some have seen the significance of the scene aptly as a confirmation of the angel's words, as well as a confirmation of an actually physical (if mysterious) Resurrection: Jesus speaks, but also can be recognized, and His feet may be seized. In this sense, the focus of the short passage is on Jesus Himself and the reality of the Resurrection. However, this unique vignette also speaks of the enormous privilege of these women as the first to see the risen Lord, and of their dominical commissioning to tell this good news. As mediators, they will tell the apostles what they have been commanded, not only by an angel, but by the LORD Himself. As mediators, they communicate to the reader the appropriate attitude (fear and joy), posture (prostration), action (coming to Jesus and seizing hold of Him), and obedient response—for they do as asked. No doubt the evangelist's first purpose was Christological, but there is also an ecclesial element, in the raising of the women to this task, for they had humbled themselves. And part of their message is ecclesial, as well: Jesus tells them to name the disciples "my brothers." One scholar puts the effect of their commission in this way: "Women emerge as solidifying agents within this new community. They are part of the reason for its existence and continuation."[18] It would seem that we should go even

---

[18]M. J. Selvidge, "Violence, Woman, and the Future of the Matthean Community: A Redactional Critical Study," *Union Seminary Quarterly Review* 39 (1984): 220.

beyond this, since they are not only centering agents, but catalyzing ones, entrusted with a primary task. Against the norms of the day, in which the witness of a woman would have been discounted, they have been told not to be afraid to assume this role. Of the two Marys, one appears to be single, and the other married with children—whether Matthew has in mind Jesus' Mother as a step-mother for Joseph's older children, or another woman who is mother of a different James and Joses. In taking on this role, each of them, in different social stations, assumes both the role of helper to the apostles and the role of Mother to the Church. Paul will not mention them in the official list of those who saw the risen Christ (1 Cor 15); yet theirs is the honor of first word, first sight, and first naming of the siblings of Christ.

In the light of these three examples, I wonder greatly at the critique of one scholar that in the New Testament Rahab is coopted as an example artificially and in James she appears "lock[ed] up in . . . theology."[19] Surely, instead, she is allowed a wonderful depth of being in which numerous facets of her person become a living pattern for those who follow her. Similarly, it seems astonishing to me that some readers of Matthew have spoken of the "flatness" of the women's characters with "nothing remarkable" narrated about them[20]— the Canaanite woman, flat? The Canaanite woman, unremarkable? (Jesus certainly did not think so!) I am equally flummoxed by another commentator who opines, "I am quite sure that women followers of Jesus were far more important and active than Matthew is letting on."[21] More important than being an ancestor of the Messiah? More important than being apostles-to-the-apostles? That same

---

[19]Ronald Charles, "Rahab: A Righteous Whore in James," *Neotestamentica* 45.2 (2011): 213.

[20]P. J. J. Botha, "The Gospel of Matthew and Women," *In die Skriflig* 37.3 (2003): 517.

[21]Botha, "The Gospel," 507.

commentator remarks, "The relevance of the women for the plot is determined by 'serving'. . . and 'worship.'[22] That is true, but perhaps we should extend that insight so that we come to see that their serving and their worship does not simply fill in and drive the plot, but it is placed there as a pattern for *all* followers of Jesus, whatever gender. Serving and worshipping aright are not light things.

Indeed, if we look closely at all of the mediating women whom we observe in this Gospel, we may see yet another aspect to their aid. One scholar demonstrates that, in general, "Matthew's pattern of righteousness may be called 'prophetic' in the classical sense: as going directly against the prevailing conduct of the secular world."[23] Surely, the holy boldness of Rahab, of the unnamed Canaanite, and of the two Marys leads them to a kind of "forth-telling" which is consonant with our understanding of prophecy. Rahab speaks truth about the God of the Hebrews; the Canaanite acknowledges, before her Gentile friends and others, the identity of this exalted "Son of David"; and the Marys utter the joyful message of the Resurrection in Matthew's Gospel, just as Mary the Mother of Jesus uttered a prophetic word concerning the Child in her womb.[24] This particular quality of maternal mediation may remind us of the way in which St Paul describes the mediating quality of the Holy Spirit in the second half of Romans 8—as a kind of spiritual midwifery that groans *with* the rest of creation, bringing Christ's new creation to birth. Without calling the Holy Spirit "she" (as some are tempted, but which Jesus

[22]Botha, "The Gospel," 514.

[23]Hagner, "Holiness," 56

[24]Mary's Magnificat is, of course, famously placed in the early pages of Luke's Gospel. But it is interesting, when we take the story of Jesus synoptically, that both at the Incarnation and at the Resurrection, God proclaims to womankind the "joy" elicited by His actions among the human race: *Rejoice, for the Lord is with you!* (Lk 1.28, 47; cf. Mt 28.9).

precludes by His use of the *masculine* pronoun for the Spirit in John 14–17),[25] we can nevertheless see a link between the internal way in which the Spirit mediates, and the way in which these women speak for God. On these grounds, we may contemplate the suggestion of Paul Evdokimov that godly women may be seen picturing the prophetic impulse given by the Holy Spirit, whereas men typically have a more priestly charism.[26]

In reading the Gospel of Matthew, there are two extremes to avoid, it seems. The first is to see the Gospel simply as a one-dimensional code that presents a doctrine of Christ, rather than a full-blown narrative with various dimensions and concerns. The second is to come at it with a contemporary "hermeneutics of suspicion,"

[25]The natural gender for the Greek word *to pneuma* is neuter, but Jesus several times uses the masculine demonstrative *ekeinos* in order to speak of the Spirit in this discourse with the disciples. Of course, Jesus was speaking Aramaic, which, like Hebrew, uses a feminine noun for Spirit (*rukha, ruach*). This is not to say that they conceived of the Spirit as feminine; yet it is the case that in Romans 8 and some Syrian poetry feminine metaphors are used to suggest the Spirit's mysterious action. All this being said, we are not wise to speculate regarding the exact wording that Jesus used at that last time with His disciples prior to His death, but rather to receive the Fourth Gospel as it stands for the purposes of our instruction on theology. If the evangelist had thought a *feminine* cast was an appropriate way to speak of the Spirit, he would have found a way to communicate it. Clearly, he thinks it necessary to clarify that Jesus is not speaking about a force but a divine Person. It is this function that is played by the surprising use of *ekeinos*. We may make a link between the Spirit and the mediating action of women without exaggeration, or dubbing the Spirit "she," against the practice of the LORD Himself.

[26]Paul Evdokimov, *Woman and the Salvation of the World: A Christian Anthropology on the Charisms of Women* (Crestwood, NY: St Vladimir's Press, 1994), 152–57; 258–59. This is not to endorse all that this theologian suggests, which is quite speculative.

assuming that we will find unrelieved patriarchy, and no interest in women for their own sake. To be sure, the truth about Jesus—Son of Man, Son of David, and Son of God—is highlighted by the evangelist. To be sure, ancients held different cultural expectations than we do about women and their role in society. But the Gospel has something to say not only about the Christ, but also about the women who take a remarkable (and remarked upon) place in Jesus' story. As matriarchs, mothers, and mediators, they tell us a good deal about Christ, even relaying the *sine qua non,* the essential event of the Resurrection. En route to that bright morning, their appearances tell us a good deal about human and divine love, as well as about the nature of the Church, whose mediating members are called both to bear their own burdens, while also bearing the burdens of others, with joy and in the fear of the Lord.

## Through the Theotokos

In the ongoing experience of the Church, there is one person who excels in glory, who specializes in intercession, and who even leads the cosmic praises of God. For generations Christians have not only called her blessed, but the Theotokos (God-bearer) and our Mother as well. Numerous examples could be given of this understanding in traditions both East and West, but perhaps it is best summarized in this resurrectional hymn:[27]

---

[27]It is helpful to remember that a "hymn" is simply a song of praise, not necessarily directed towards God or a god. Classical Christian hymns distinguish the appropriate *kind* of praise given to God or to a saint, as suggested by St John of Damascus in his treatise on the icons.

> You who were the mediatrix of the salvation of
>    our race,
> we hymn, Virgin Theotokos!
> For in the flesh, that very flesh taken from you,
> your Son and our God,
> because he had embraced the passion of the cross,
> redeemed us from corruption, as the Lover of
>    Mankind.[28]

The hymn addresses the Virgin Mary, beginning with the pronoun "you." We return to the initial problem of our study: in the New Covenant, each of us is promised a direct relationship with God, each of us is filled with the Holy Spirit, each of us is promised illumination. As the prophet Jeremiah promised, *And no longer shall each man teach his neighbor and each his brother, saying, "Know the LORD," for they shall all know me, from the least of them to the greatest* (Jer 31.34, RSV). Jeremiah caught a glimpse of our time in which all of God's people would see, and not be kept in the dark, or have less knowledge than various anointed prophets, priests, and kings, upon whom (under the Old Covenant) the Holy Spirit almost exclusively fell. And yet, as we have seen, in the New Covenant we still care for each other, still pray for each other, still teach each other, still help each other, still bear each other's burdens. So it is that the ancient Church kept the office of priest, and that bishops were anointed who succeeded the apostles, those who initially had seen the risen Jesus with their own eyes. Alongside the Twelve the ancient Church has, even in its liturgies, celebrated the holy Birthgiver and Mother of God, crying out, "Holy Theotokos, come to our aid!"

---

[28]Orthodox Resurrectional Troparion, Tone 3, my translation.

So we come face to face with this term *Mediatrix*, startling to many who are no longer aware of the Latin feminine ending used for a title of function, which used to be recognized in other contexts—a male "executor" of a will, but a female "executrix," for example. "Mediatrix," then, in the feminine form, is added to the term "Mediator," as part of the Christian family vocabulary. It is not, of course, found specifically in the New Testament. But neither is the word "Trinity." Her role, however, is both described in the New Testament and prefigured in the Old Testament at various points. It should be emphasized that the term "Mediatrix" and the title "Redemptrix" are very different: the Orthodox Church is not tempted to call Mary our "Co-redemptrix," unlike some pious Roman Catholics who have appealed to the pope several times to formally approve of this title (so far, unsuccessfully). This distinction is apparent in the hymn, which speaks of Mary as the Mediatrix, but of Jesus alone as the one who "redeemed" humanity from corruption. Indeed, the hymn follows a typical pattern in Orthodox worship, which honors the Virgin Mary, only to immediately turn to Christ in worship and commitment.

As this hymn expresses it, then, Mary has mediated for us in a particular and powerful way, but it is the Son alone who "redeemed us" through the cross. It is, after all, the Theotokos who historically brought this One into our midst, for He took flesh from her alone (without a human father), and in that flesh suffered on the cross. In that distinct sense, she mediated our salvation: thus the hymn puts her decisive action in the past tense when it says "you. . . *were* the mediatrix." The prophet Isaiah, it seems, saw a symbolic preview of her mediating role in a vision. In the sixth chapter of his prophecy, we hear how he saw the ineffable God high and lifted up, and one of the angels of God's presence flew to him with a live coal held with tongs. The angel touched this coal to his lips, cleansing him, and preparing him to speak. In Orthodox hymnody, this visionary image is likened to the great honor given to St Symeon, who received the "living Coal"—Jesus, the divine Child—in the Temple, given to him from the Virgin Mary's arms, arms "like tongs" that offered this cleansing child to the righteous old man.[29]

Some visitors, when first entering an Orthodox church, are distracted by a huge representation of the Virgin Mary in the curved apse, and wonder why she is so prominent. If they look closer, however, they will notice that she is not alone there, but holds Christ out in her arms. It is as if she is saying to us, as she said to Symeon, "Here He is!" As if she is saying to us, as she did to the servers at Cana, "Do whatever He tells you!" As if she is saying to us, as she did to Elisabeth, "My soul magnifies God my Savior! You rejoice, too!" Her greatest act of mediation, then, comes by virtue of who she is: the Mother, Bearer, and Birthgiver of God the Son. Icons of this holy woman invariably show her with her Son, for it is to Him that she directs us. Indeed, one of the most common and ancient icons of the Virgin Mary is known as the *Hodēgētria*, a title that literally means "she who shows the way." In this icon, which is often attributed in its origins to the evangelist Luke, her hand points to her Son, who is Himself the Way. When Christians honor her as the "Mother of God," they are making a statement that is as much about Him as her: there is *one* Christ, the indivisible God-Man, whose mother she was. It is not sufficient, then, to call her "the Mother of Jesus" as a

---

[29]Various Orthodox hymns use this image, but the most poignant, in my opinion, is that sung in the Small Vespers service for the Feast of the Presentation in the Temple "Christ the coal of fire, whom holy Isaiah foresaw, now rests in the arms of the Theotokos as a pair of tongs, and He is given to the elder. With fear and joy Symeon held the Master in his arms, and asked for his relief from life, singing the praises of the Mother of God."

substitute for "the Mother of God." Charles Wesley makes a similar move when he cries, "Amazing love! How can it be that thou my *God* should'st die for me?" If Jesus is truly God, then God died. If Jesus is truly God, then Mary is the Mother of God (incarnate)—not, of course, the mother of the Father or the mother of the Holy Spirit. Moreover, if she is the Mother of our LORD, then she is our Mother as well!

Those of us who come to *know* her as Mother (like St John the Evangelist, cf. Jn 19.26) honor her in the first place for her unique part in bringing the Savior into the world. Yet we also come to realize that her mediation is not limited to this historical and crucial role as the one from whom Jesus took flesh: rather, it is ongoing. Here, some will realize, this study moves beyond the Church's public proclamation of Christ, and into the interior experience of God's family. I consider, though, that any who have persisted this far in our study of mediation have some interest in what Christians in the historic Church think about such matters. In probing what we remember of the LORD's Mother, we must not expect to find it detailed in the Scriptures (which focus on Jesus), but rather discovered in the witness of God's people to their corporate life—though we may at least get a sense of her important place even in the earliest community of New Testament believers.

## Endings and Beginnings, Her Death and Birth

After all, Luke makes it clear that she was with the Apostles in those early days of the Church, in the upper room, at Pentecost and at the Ascension. (In Acts 1.14, she is noted explicitly, and separately from the other women.) It would seem that the solemn gift that Jesus gave from the cross to His beloved disciple—the gift of a mother—had been generalized to the other disciples, in whose company she was now found. Tradition tells us that when she "fell asleep," that is, when she died, almost all the apostles were present, honoring her— though poor St Thomas was delayed, as at the Resurrection! This time, though, his delay ushered in joy for the entire community, since on asking to see where they had laid her, he perceived, with the others, that her body was no longer there. The ancient Tradition of the Church then, is not that she was assumed bodily without dying like Enoch and Elijah into God's presence, but that she experienced the end common to humanity, that of death, and her body was honored in a special way, so that she was restored body and soul into the presence of God, as a sign that this is the future of all who are in Christ.[30] That there are no actual relics of the body claimed to be guarded anywhere in the world, but only her *zōnē*, or belt, tacitly suggests that this tradition regarding her bodily glorification is very early. One would expect, in a Christian community that boasts of so many relics, that

[30]Our first extant record of the Dormition is about AD 330 in an artifact (a picture on a sarcophagus) discovered in Spain. Cf. Lilian H. Zirpolo, *Historical Dictionary of Baroque Art and Architecture* (Washington, DC: Rowan and Littlefield, 2018), 213. The story is found in various apocryphal writings (e.g., *The Protoevangelium of James*) and liturgical hymns. Some Roman Catholics maintain that Mary did not die, but was only assumed, but a careful reading of the dogmatic statement *Munificentissimus Deus* will note the implication that she died, and Pope John Paul II explicitly declared this in an audience that he gave in 1997, https://www.vatican.va/content/john-paul-ii/en/audiences/1997/documents/hf_jp-ii_aud_25061997.html (Retrieved April 2022). Confirming his informal statement in that audience is the Roman Catholic Catechism itself, which in paragraph 966 quotes the ancient troparion in which the Theotokos is said to have undergone "dormition" ("falling asleep," or death): " In giving birth you kept your virginity, in *your Dormition* you did not leave the world, O Mother of God, but were joined to the source of Life."

any personal relics of the Mother of God would have been proudly claimed. Yet there are no such claims, nor any past reports of them.

The ancient Church, then, has both remembered her Dormition (her "falling asleep") and celebrated her glorification or exaltation with Christ. In her very person she becomes an icon of what Christians can hope for, as those who are redeemed. All who are baptized into Christ's death anticipate resurrection and glory; the Virgin Mary, at Jesus' right hand, is a tangible sign of this. As the first after Christ to be raised, in hymnody she assumes chief place, supplanting even the angels who orchestrate worship, and so leads the great host of witnesses that cheers us on (Heb 12.1). Joyful in the presence of her Son, she helps us to stay the course. Not only the East but also the West recognizes her in this role, addressing her as "more honorable than the cherubim and more glorious beyond compare than the seraphim," a leader of the cosmic choir.[31] C. S. Lewis uses this helpful picture to help us recapture the ancient view that we are members one of the other:

> Human beings look separate because you see them walking about separately. But then we are so made that we can see only the present moment. If we could see the past, then of course it would look different. For there was a time when every man was part of his mother, and (earlier still) part of his father as well, and when they were part of his grandparents. If you could see humanity spread out in time, as God sees it, it would look like

---

[31]This is ubiquitous in Orthodox worship, but can also be found in an Anglican hymn: "O, higher than the cherubim, more glorious than the seraphim / Lead their praises / Alleluia!" This is the second verse of a hymn written in the early twentieth century by Athelstan Riley, itself a translation of the Latin hymn *Vigiles et Sancti*. The English hymn was first published in 1906, and is found in standard Anglican hymnals.

one single growing thing—rather like a very complicated tree.
Every individual would appear connected with every other.[32]

Somehow, then, we are persons, distinct from each other, and also
joined together, biologically and chronologically. Mary, the Mother
of Jesus, was distinct in her context, in her upbringing, in her per-
sonality, and in the way that God used her for our salvation. Yet, as
Mother of God, and as Mother bequeathed to the Church, she also is
intimately connected with each of us. It is this conviction concerning
human solidarity that made it possible for the earliest Christians to
grasp the significance of remaining "in Adam" or being baptized into
the *new* Adam, into Christ. Similarly, we are bound to Eve, or now
keep company with the new Eve, the one who said "Yes!" to God,
rather than heeding the demonic challenge, "Did God say?" (see
Lk 1.38; Gen 3.1). Any person, by virtue of his or her humanity, may
now be baptized into Christ, or, to keep Lewis's metaphor, become a
branch in the true Tree or Vine. Though God began by teaching the
Hebrew people in particular about Him, this was so that they would
be a light to *the whole world*: Christ came for the *human race*, and not
simply for Israel. This is the point subtly made by the evangelist Matthew, who in his first chapter includes Gentile women as part of the
family tree of Joseph, the betrothed of Mary.

It is by means of a young woman who found high favor with God
that Christ came, and in a unique manner: "Without corruption [she]
gave birth to God the Word!"[33] Some who are cynical may be tempted
to see in this a criticism of human sexual and generative activity, as

[32]C. S. Lewis, *Mere Christianity*, 161.

[33]This is a well-known phrase from the hymn to the Theotokos called "It
is truly meet. . ." (*Axion estin).* It is sung prominently in the Divine Liturgy
after the consecration of the gifts, but also elsewhere in Orthodox worship
(e.g., it forms part of the dismissal sequence at the end of nearly every service).

though human intercourse in itself brings corruption, or giving birth in itself brings uncleanness to the woman. Others may assume this is a reference to Mary's moral holiness, and that the hymn is asserting that she was in a state of moral purity when she gave birth to Jesus. (Orthodox, of course, proclaim her all-holiness, while maintaining that in absolute terms, Jesus is the "only sinless One.") But it would seem that the phrase "without corruption" has a very specific sense in this hymn. We remember that Eve, as a result of the Fall, was consigned by God to give birth in pain, as a reminder of her dependence and fragility (just as Adam was consigned to do manual labor with difficulty). Part of that "pain" involved the violation of her body, its tearing as she labored, just as Adam's labor would bring wounds, callouses, and the like. Of course, ever since the Fall, loving husbands and wives have shared each other's wounds and hardships, either physically or psychologically.

But the Mediatrix did not, says the Tradition, bring the Savior into the world in that way: He came as a gentleman, not harming her womb or her birth canal. After all, *her* pain was to come later, the sword piercing her as He died on the cross (cf. Lk 2.35). As for His coming into the world, it happened in such a way that Eve's woe may clearly be seen to be *undone*. His mother Mary, like the myrrh-bearers, cast away the ancestral curse, and brought her firstborn, God's Only Begotten, into the world in a moment of sheer joy, without any woe. Surely this gentle birthing is an apt picture of what was happening on a cosmic level at that moment. The incarnate God, the Rescuer, came to His own to redeem them, not to wound them: the suffering would be His to bear, at the appropriate time, and it would undo sin, death, and corruption. *When the time had fully come, God sent forth His Son, born of woman . . . to redeem us . . . that we might receive adoption as sons* (Gal 4.4–5). In complete solidarity with us, Jesus has a human parent, one who has brought into the midst of humanity that one who is the Redeemer from sin, corruption, and death. Since this is His role alone, it would not be fitting that Mary should suffer as humanity received this gift.

## *Like Son, Like Mother: Ongoing Mediation and Many Names*

Just as the salvation of the LORD is ongoing, so the Church has understood the mediation of the saints as continuing, especially the mediation of Mary, and it has pictured this in exuberant metaphors. In order to show the breadth of contemplation associated with this Mediatrix, we will fasten upon another hymn of the Church:

> Most precious Virgin,
> you are the gate, the temple,
> the palace, the throne of the King.
> From you, my Redeemer, Christ the Lord, appeared
> to those asleep in darkness.
> He is the Sun of Righteousness,
> who desired to enlighten His image, whom He had
> created.
> Since you possess motherly boldness before Him, all
> praised Lady,
> pray unceasingly that our souls may be saved![34]

Pray unceasingly, the hymn asks! With this image, her mediation becomes a model for what Christians are called to do for each other: *to always pray, and never to lose heart* (Luke 18.1). In her person, and in this role, we see the communion of saints.

---

[34]Theotokion at the Aposticha, Saturday Evening Vespers (Octoechos, Tone 5).

This hymn hides its depth in seeming simplicity. In it several images from the Old Testament call attention to the unique place of the Virgin Mary in God's economy of salvation. Here she is called the Gate, the Temple, the Palace, and the Throne of the King. As we encounter this series of pictures, we may recall old Jerusalem, in the city's heyday under King Solomon, when she was a glorious walled city, set on high, and ornamented with both a Temple and a Palace. The Psalms and Prophets are replete with references to the gates of Jerusalem: *The LORD loves the gates of Zion more than all the habitations of Jacob* (Ps 86.2, LXX); *Enter into His gates with thanksgiving, and His courts with praise: be thankful unto Him, and bless His name* (Ps 99.4, LXX); *Our feet shall stand within your gates, O Jerusalem* (Ps 121.2, LXX); *Praise the LORD, O Jerusalem; praise your God, O Zion. For He has strengthened the bars of your gates; He has blessed your children within you. He makes peace in your borders* (Ps 147.12–14, LXX); *Open the gates, so that the righteous nation that is faithful may enter in, because they hope forever in You, O Lord* (Is 26.2–3).

This final verse from Isaiah reminds us of the purpose of "gates"— they are a way in, of course, but they are also a continuation of the surrounding wall, to protect the faithful and to keep out the violent who do not belong. In ancient times, too, gates were a natural gathering place, as we hear in the Old Testament, where the judge sat in court at the gates, handling disputes, or where inhabitants gathered to exchange news. Of the virtuous woman it is said, *Give to her from the fruit of her hands; and let her husband praise her at the gates* (Prov 31.31). When Jerusalem was rebuilt in the time of Nehemiah, it appears that it had ten gates (we can count them in several Old Testament books); there may have been twelve in Jesus' day. Certainly, the apostle and prophet John had a vision of a time when there would be twelve glorious gates, representing the fullness of God's people (like the twelve tribes, or twelve apostles, cf. Rev 21.21). Indeed, in that glad day, when all rebellion has been quelled, there will be no need to shut the gates, either by day or night, but all who come in will do so to bring glory to God (Is 60.11; Rev 21.24–25). As the prophet exults, *Violence shall no more be heard in your land, nor wasting or destruction within your borders; but you shall call your walls Salvation, and your gates Praise* (Is 60.18).

So then, the gates provide an entrance for all who belong in the holy city. But, of course, in our hymn, the Virgin Mary is called *the* gate, just as Jesus is called "the way." There is something singular, or special, about the *entrance* that she gave to the incarnate LORD, and that she gives to those who seek God's presence. Jesus entered the city of Jerusalem by the East (or Beautiful) Gate, which was blocked by the sultan Suleiman the Magnificent centuries later. The prophet Ezekiel (in chapters 44–46) foresees the gate being sealed, and refers to the uniqueness of the king who will enter through this gate, so that it would not be appropriate for another to use it. The Church has taken these passages to refer not primarily to a physical sealing of the Temple entrance, but rather to the ever-virginity of Mary.[35] We

---

[35]Mary's ongoing virginity after the birth of Jesus was generally undisputed in the Church prior to the time of the Reformation, with a few exceptions in the first five centuries (marginal groups known as the "antidicomarianites" and Helvidius, against whom Jerome wrote). After this we see no evidence of controversy concerning the doctrine, and indeed it was accepted by the famous Reformers Calvin, Luther, and even Zwingli, who did not consider the reference to "brothers and sisters" in the New Testament to refer to Mary's own children. Roman Catholics appeal to the extended meaning of "brother" in ancient culture to refer to relatives; Orthodox maintain that Joseph had children such as St James from an earlier marriage. This is not the place to arbitrate between these views, nor to defend what was an uncontested doctrine of the Church for 1,600 years. What should not be gathered from the teaching is that Christianity considers sexual activity "impure" (see Heb 13.4);

are meant to picture the entrance from her holy womb as the portal uniquely taken by the infant LORD, so that our Savior could come into the midst of humanity. With this image we go back to her foundational mediating role, as the gate of the one who is our Salvation. The Psalmist's joy seems an apt response: *This is the gate of the LORD, by which the righteous shall enter. I will praise Thee: for thou hast heard me, and have become my salvation* (Ps 117.19–21, LXX).

She is the gate, but she is also, suggests the hymn, the Temple. The constructed Temple, of course, was not originally God's idea, but that of the man David. By the prophet, God reminds us, indeed, of the impossibility of "containing" Him: *Heaven is my throne, and the earth is my footstool; what is the house that you would build for me, and what is the place of my rest?* (Is 66.1, RSV). Yet He condescended to meet with His people at the mercy seat, the Ark in the Temple that prefigured that greater place of meeting, when God's time for a deeper visitation had fully come. It is the Virgin Mary, a human being made by God, and not by human hands, who would become the *living* shrine of the God-Man, holding physically within her the Savior of the world. If we stop to think about this, we can scarcely take it in, and will understand why some have exclaimed that her womb became "more spacious than the heavens"—ample enough, by God's grace, to contain the uncontainable LORD!

In this image, she offers a picture of what each of us hopes to become—living shrines of the Lord, offering His life to others. As Jesus promised, *Whoever drinks of the water that I will give will never be thirsty again. The water that I will give to that one will become in him*

---

rather, Mary's perpetual virginity is a sign of her special consecration as Theotokos, the bearer of the unique God-Man. One has only to imagine oneself in the place of Joseph to decide whether it might be presumptuous to inhabit the same place as God Himself.

*a spring of water welling up to eternal life* (Jn 4.14). Of course, Mary alone "bore" Jesus as a mother bears a child, enshrining Him in her womb, and bringing forth for us the one who is our Salvation. Yet the Christian Tradition has spoken of the possibility that all of us may "bear" Him in different ways, carrying His life within us so that others may see it: *We are the fragrance of Christ among those who are being saved* (2 Cor 2.15). Indeed, some of the earliest commentators of the book of Revelation (Hippolytus, St Andrew of Caesarea) understood the picture of the woman giving birth to the Messiah as a picture specifically of God's people, since the "bearing" takes place with anguish, and not in the quiet manner of Mary's birthing (Rev 12.2). The popularity of the name "Christopher" (literally, "Christ-bearer") also attests to this role, to which each of us is called. Mary may be the unique bearer in terms of giving birth, as she was, quite literally, "the way" by which the LORD came among us. Yet all Christians are called to "lift high the cross!" as the Western hymn puts it, and so carry Christ in a different way. This sacrificial carrying is famously exemplified by the early martyr St Ignatius, who thus encouraged his followers: "You . . . are God-bearers, temple-bearers, Christ-bearers, bearers of holiness" (Eph 9). Together, we are the holy ones, the "temple" of the living God—a tangible and physical sign of God's presence in the world.

She is also called "the palace." When it was in its prime, Jerusalem had a Temple for the LORD and a palace for the King. The king's palace was never seen as something that should overshadow the glory of God, but it was understood to exist because of God's favor and clemency. Indeed, David reasoned with God that is seemed impertinent for *him* to have a royal house, while the LORD was worshipped in an impermanent, moveable tabernacle (2 Sam/2 Kingdoms 7.2). God had no need for this man-made construction, but eventually allowed Solomon to build a temple for Him—and the king saw to it that the Temple was more glorious than his palace. The LORD alone was to be worshipped, and the king's glory depended upon the God who had anointed him. We see this same emphasis in a visionary book called *1 Enoch*, where we hear about two buildings: "Then that house [the palace of the king] became great and spacious . . . and a lofty and great tower [the Temple] was built on the house for the Lord; that house was low, but the tower was really elevated and lofty, and the Lord . . . stood upon that tower and they offered a full table before Him" (*1 Enoch* 89.50).[36] Indeed, when we remember that Jesus is King of kings, it seems appropriate to unite the images of Temple (where He made atonement for our salvation, and where He meets with us) and Palace (where we see Him in all His glory). Isaiah's "throne-room" vision catches a glimpse of the LORD in a Temple-Palace, on His throne!

Let us turn to the final picture of the Theotokos in this hymn: she is the "throne" of the LORD. It is in this role that we see her in many icons, her arms encircling Him as an armchair encircles the one who sits upon it. The throne is the focal point of the palace, just as the Ark of the Covenant is in the central and most important place of the Temple. It is helpful to remember that the Ark was not only the chest that contained the relics of the people of Israel (the manna, Aaron's budding rod, and so on), but also served as a kind of "seat" for the invisible God of Israel, and was surrounded by representations of adoring cherubim, curving around it. The Ark, then represented the "throne" of God in the humanly built Temple, and was also called "the footstool" where He promised to meet the people. Isaiah suggests that this Temple-throne was a representation of something so glorious we can scarcely imagine it: *I saw the LORD sitting on a throne, high and lifted up. The house was full of His*

---

[36]Translation by E. Isaac, in *Old Testament Pseudepigrapha*, vol. 1, ed. James H. Charlesworth (New York: Doubleday, 1983), 67.

*glory* (Is 6.1). It is in this vision that God's glory is celebrated by the seraphim (seemingly of an even higher order than the cherubim), who cry the thrice-holy hymn; it is in this vision that Isaiah understands his sin, and the sin of Israel; it is in this vision that the prophet is touched by the living coal, cleansed, and commissioned; and it is in this vision that both the desolation and restoration of Israel are promised.

The prophet understood what the book of Hebrews makes clear—that the earthly Temple (and palace) with its throne, are only copies or representations of a realm that we cannot yet see, but into which Jesus has gone ahead, preparing a place for us. He has entered for us as our High Priest into the true holy place, and so made it possible for us to draw near even now in worship to the heavenly Mount Zion, joining *the church of the firstborn whose names are enrolled in heaven* (Heb 12.23). When we worship, gathering together, we have a potent foretaste of how we will rejoice with patriarchs, matriarchs, prophets, apostles, virgins, prophetesses, archangels, angels, cherubim, seraphim, and beloved Mary, who is "the gate, the temple, the palace, and the throne of the King." In past ages, humanly crafted cherubim guarded the Ark in the Temple as the earthly throne of the LORD. After the Temple was desolated by the Babylonians, the living cherubim brought God's mystical celestial throne in a vision to the prophet Ezekiel, who languished in exile with the Jewish people in Babylon. But now, we celebrate the time when the Virgin's womb "became [or supplanted] the throne of the cherubim," and "heaven was found in a cave!"[37] The best humanity has to offer, Mary, is the human throne upon whom the Lord is exalted, and as

[37]These luminous phrases are from St John Damascus, from the Irmos for the Ninth Ode of the Matins Canon for the Feast of the Nativity of Christ (Menaion, December 25).

we sing with her, *He is enthroned* eternally *on the praises* of His people (Ps 22.3, in the Hebrew).

As is apt in prayer and worship, while this hymn that has structured our meditation invites us to picture Jesus' Mother in numerous ways, it ultimately leads us to worship *Him*: "From you (Mary), my Redeemer, Christ the Lord, appeared to those asleep in darkness. He is the Sun of Righteousness, who desired to enlighten His image, whom He had created." The hymn is addressed to the Theotokos, but climaxes with the Lord of all. This pattern follows the norm for Orthodox worship, which frequently calls to remembrance our "all-holy . . . Lady Theotokos," but then firmly "commend[s] . . . all our life to Christ our God." While in the Old Testament the Lord met mysteriously with His people, occasionally signaling His presence in cloud and fire, now the God-Man meets His people as the King, as the Priest, and as the Sacrifice for all! He alone is "the Sun of Righteousness," and so the Virgin Mary delights to turn to Him in hope, interceding with her Son for us, as our Mother, too. It is with that intercession, appropriate for a Mother who can be "bold" with her Son, Lord though He is, that the hymn closes. We remember that holy boldness as a characteristic displayed among the women of Matthew's Gospel—asking the spies for protection, being importunate with Jesus, breaking cultural convention to inform the apostles of the Resurrection. Moreover, boldness is something that all Christians may adopt (so long as it does not banish our reverence): as St Paul puts it in 2 Corinthians 3.12, *Since we have such a hope, we are bold.* The very prayer that Jesus taught us informs us that we may be bold to say, to our very Creator, "Our Father." Yet, we especially mark this confidence in the comportment of His Mother, as she speaks with Him at the wedding at Cana (Jn 2), and in the transparent interchange between the two at that time. From her we learn that we may approach Him, for He is good and loves us. And when we are not strong enough, we ask for her forthright and enlightened prayers, for He has given her to us as our Mother, too.

In writing this way about my beloved Mother in the LORD, I am aware of some vulnerability. As mentioned at the start of this section, these words about the Theotokos are not properly part of the public proclamation of the Church, which focuses upon the God-Man, Jesus. They are rather a major feature in our family ways, our inner experience, and as such are dear and intimate matters. It may well be that some who are reading these lines find them challenging, improbable, or even impious, since not everyone who names Jesus has been nurtured according to these ancient memories. Perhaps it is helpful to know that a friendship with the Virgin Mary is not simply a doctrine to be talked about, but a relationship that needs to be cultivated, in the company of those who also know her. Going to our Lady in times of extremity, and also on a comfortable daily basis, are ways to approach this exalted and humble one, to learn from her example, and to benefit from her ongoing care for the children whom Jesus has given to her. It has been helpful for many of us to pray the Akathist (literally "Standing") prayers to the Theotokos with others during worship, and also to keep handy the "sweet-kissing" icon of Jesus, which portrays Him in intimate contact with His Mother. That intimacy which He had with her is our birthright, as His brothers and sisters. The Mediatrix does not act as a door to bar the way, but as one with glowing arms who lifts Him out to us. Her strong presence in the Christian community puts aside the charge of those today who dismiss Christianity as a "man's religion." Instead, it is the living faith of the One who came to us through a young woman, who showed by her life what He means to do for all who come to love Him, whether male or female. The inner tenderness of the family home (as it is meant to be!) combines with the mysterious awe of the heavenly Temple:

> Welcome, all wonders in one sight!
> Eternity shut in a span;
> Summer in winter; day in night;
> Heaven in earth, and God in Man!
> Brave little One, whose all-embracing birth
> Lifts earth to heaven, stoops heav'n to earth![38]

[38]Richard Crashaw, "In the Holy Nativity of Our Lord," *The Complete Poetry of Richard Crashaw*, ed. George W. Williams (New York University Press, 1972).

# Meant to be Mediators

Though this study began with the premise that mediation is best understood as a characteristic of God's *people*, by which they show God's generosity, our explorations have led us down many paths, including those that are not strictly within the human realm. Both our common experience down through the ages and direct teaching from the Scriptures and the Church Fathers indicate that we must hold together two halves of a mystery: each of us is called to a personal and *immediate* relationship with the LORD; that relationship comes to us, paradoxically, *by way of mediation*. Especially this mediation is seen as operative within the Body of Christ, but it also embraces those who are not yet among us. We have two hopes: to be authentic members within the household of God, and to know Him by entering, with others, into the mysterious communion of the Father, Son, and Holy Spirit. In all this, we are called together to be mediators, and to accept the mediation of others, both with regard to those living and those in the eternal presence of the LORD. Authentic mediation is not a Christian form of magic, nor a way of manipulating God, but rather we always engage in mediation so as to glorify the great Mediator, the God-Man. In the words of Richard of Chichester, we pray so as to see Him more clearly, follow Him more nearly, and love Him more dearly, day by day.

Our prayers as the Body of Christ are shaped, then, by His great mediation, demonstrating both our dependence upon Him and our love for others. Early in the history of the Church, Christian artists portrayed a practice in prayer that is also described by the early theologian Tertullian (c. 160–220)—the "Orans" posture (literally "the Praying One"): "We not only lift them [our hands] up, but also spread them out, and, modulating them by the Lord's passion, in our prayers also express our faith in Christ."[1] Over a hundred and fifty representations of this mode of prayer are found on tombs and walls in the Catacombs, representing, it seems, the ongoing prayers of those who have died for their living brothers and sisters. While some of these supplicating figures are well-known Old Testament leaders such as Abraham, Daniel, and the three youths in the furnace, many of the depictions are idealized and female, underscoring the insight that we have drawn in this study, that mediation is the purview of every Christian. Indeed, we may gather, from the strong appearance of female figures on male tombs, that the soul itself is depicted as female, crying out, like the Bride in the last chapter of Revelation, *Even so, come Lord Jesus* (22.20). Some of the better known Orans images take on the appearance of the Theotokos herself, as her special mediation comes to the fore. The Orans, used as a posture for prayer, and depicted in the place where the earliest persecuted Christians were buried, is a potent reminder of the mediating character of God's people, who pattern themselves on the humility of Christ, lift out hands in supplication for others, and long for His return to fulfill all things.

---

[1]Tertullian, *De Oratione* 14; translation in *Tertullian: Disciplinary, Moral, and Ascetical Works*, trans. Rudolph Arbesmann, Emily Joseph Daly, and Edwin A. Quain, Fathers of the Church 40 (Washington, DC: The Catholic University of America Press, 1962), 46.

Mediation is, then, neither a "frill" nor an accessory to the Christian life. It is a necessary route by which God works in us and through us. Why this is so for a sovereign God, who is free to enlarge us in whichever way He pleases, we cannot fully say. We can, however, glean reasons for His purposes from other matters that He has revealed to us. First, He delineated and separated the multiple elements of creation and called these *good* at every step (Gen 1.4, 10, 12, 18, 21, 25); then, He declared the completion of the human being, made according to His likeness, *very good* (Gen 1.31); finally, He said that it was *not good* that Adam should be alone (Gen 2.18), and so created Eve, out of a part of Adam (but not merely as his extension), thus making a family. The Fall disrupted the natural order of God's work, but it did not obliterate it: even in the curse, we see the intertwining of Adam (who must now work hard for his family), Eve (who longs for her husband and brings forth children in pain), and the rest of the created order, whom St Paul says is presently *yearning for the revelation of God's sons*, so that it, too, may be redeemed (Rom 8.22).

Indeed, we can learn much about mediation simply by looking around us. Nature itself, it seems, works by this principle—in terms that are both mutual and hierarchical. When C. S. Lewis speaks about the "Grand Miracle" of the Incarnation in his book *Miracles,* he approaches the philosophical difficulties of accepting miracles by stressing several details about reality that we often ignore or even suppress: the composite nature of humanity as body, soul, and spirit; the pattern of "descent and re-ascent" that we see in nature itself; the "selectiveness" of life that we see all around us; "vicariousness" as a way of daily life; and our call to humility in the face of a clearly hierarchical reality.[2] (To these we must add the mysterious way

---

[2]C. S. Lewis, *Miracles: A Preliminary Study* (New York: HarperOne, 1974 [1st ed. 1947]), 112–135. Cf. C. S. Lewis, *God in the Dock: Essays on Theology and*

in which those stronger members of the creation must sometimes depend upon the weaker, a truth that Lewis plays out in his novels, but does not emphasize in this chapter.) We are especially indebted to Lewis's astute perception concerning the principle of "transposition," which allows us to see that this pattern of descending to re-ascend is imprinted in nature.[3] A human being, for example, can become "doggish" with her pet: the "higher" and "greater" is able to enter into the world of the lower and smaller, for the purposes of mediation.

Armed with this nuanced description of reality, we may narrate the Christian story in such a way that mediation makes eminent sense. We may have preferred a simple story in which God simply draws the circle of welcome bigger and bigger, beginning with Israel, then with the Gentiles, and so on. (Indeed, some have generalized our family narrative so that it is limited to these optimistic contours. Yet this simplistic shaping of the Christian story paves the way for a universalist new religion, indebted to Theosophism, that has no real hope to offer those searching for a particular savior or for sexual purity of life.[4]) Instead, we have received something much more messy, a story that emphasizes elements that seem a little distasteful

---

*Ethics*, ed. Walter Hooper (Grand Rapids, MI: William B. Eerdmans Publishing Company, 2014), 76–85.

[3]Ibid., 115. The concept is worked out more fully in his celebrated essay, "Transposition," in C. S. Lewis, *The Weight of Glory: And Other Addresses* (New York: HarperOne, 2001 [1st ed. 1949]), 91–115. In fact, Lewis's concept might be better captured by the term "transcription" (rather than "transposition"), since transcription involves putting a musical piece in another less-textured idiom (for example, scaling down a symphony to a piano duet), and transposition only involves changing the key.

[4]For an example of this theological construal, see Bishop Michael Ingham, *Mansions of the Spirit: The Gospel in a Multi-faith World* (Toronto: Anglican Book Centre, 2009).

in our egalitarian age: first, the *selectivity* of God, who narrows down His focus by working in Israel, then in Judah, then in His remnant, and finally in Mary the Theotokos ("God-bearer") herself; secondly, the *vicariousness* of life, whereby we are dependent upon others, and especially on this greatest other One who took on our humanity, laying down His life for us. In a gospel that constantly surprises us, getting the balance right is not easy. How do we account fully for the difference between Creator and creation while acknowledging their interrelationship? How do we hold to a normative mode of life for that creation, as the strong interact with the weak, while also reckoning with a sovereign God who may, at His will, call upon the weak to confound the mighty? How do we rejoice in the New Covenant by which each of us may know God, while still delighting in the intimate relationships that God the Holy Spirit forges among His children, as well as between them and the angels, and between them and the rest of the created order?

It would seem that a sober estimate of our creaturely condition must be retained: we alternately depend upon some and nurture others. But we guard this humble assessment of our condition alongside the wonder that God has so made the world that it is intertwined in surprising ways: the African bush elephant is in the debt of those wee beasts that keep his tusk clean even while they are nourished by the debris they find on it. "The Circle of Life" is a gross caricature, but it captures some of the truth.

Moreover, our story is not simply a natural one, but partakes of the very glory of the Triune God. Thus, to Genesis we add Jesus' prayer for His community in John 17, that we all "be one" *as* Father, Son, and Spirit are one. Our hope is not simply for harmonious co-living such as that envisaged in Genesis 1 and 2 (though that would be a welcome return) but for actual divine communion that draws its life from God Himself. Jesus' prayer acknowledges an order in the Church, assuming that the Twelve will speak to others, who will believe because of their witness (Jn 17.20); it also acknowledges a unity that is mutual, just as the Son, who is Light-from-Light, is truly one with the Father. To take the Holy Trinity as a model is, of course, a cheeky thing! God's essence is known only to Himself, and the mode of His oneness we will never fully grasp. And yet, we are invited to make this comparison of "oneness" by Jesus' own prayers, and by His generosity to call us "friends" (not merely servants), even while we retain our state as creatures: *I no longer call you servants, for the servant does not know what the master is doing; but I have called you "friends," since everything that I have heard from my Father I have made known to you* (Jn 15.15).

Part of what Jesus has made known, indeed, is God's strange mode of revelation to us *through others,* coupled with the challenging invitation that we share in this work of mediation. So, then, mediation is both a *means* to friendship with God, and also one of those very treasures that God delights to show, not only *to* us, but *in* us. Being a friend of God is another way of typifying an "immediate" relationship. Such friendship is not instantly formed, but matures over time and with experience, as every one of us who makes a new friend knows. It is Jesus who has made us and called us friends; we have heard about this new status through those who have written Gospels, and those who have translated them; finally, we continue to explore what this friendship means within the community of believers, as other friends show us more and more concerning this "great little" One who lifts earth to heaven, having stooped heaven to earth. Living in a complex family such as this makes for humility, generosity, acknowledgement of everyone, a full-bodied reflection of Christ, the possibility of reconciliation for all, and a growing communion with each other (indeed with the entire cosmos) in which we do not lose who we are as human persons. We come not only to be friends of God in a formal sense, but to value and cherish those people and things that He loves. Both our participation in mediating, and our reception of what is mediated, open us up to the largeness, the depth, and the intricacy of the world that God has made. As another little-known poem of Richard Crashaw exclaims,

> How many unknown WORLDS there are
> Of Comforts, which Thou hast in Keeping!
> How many Thousand Mercyes there
> In Pity's soft lap lie a sleeping!
> Happy he who has the art
> To awake them
> And to take them
> Home, and lodge them in his HEART.[5]

My desire in this short study has been to pass on a partial glimpse of these many "unknown worlds" (with their hidden angelic, human, and creaturely inhabitants), and invite others into this larger world. There are many means of aid that the LORD has in His treasure-store, ready to use for our healing, strengthening, and enlargement. Indeed, it is by the "comfort," "mercy," and "pity" of the one Mediator, Christ, that *all* other mediations are made available, waiting there for us to "awaken" (or for us to wake up to?) and "take home" to our hearts. The apostle tells us that "prophecies," specific words of "knowledge," and "tongues" will cease when we see Him face to face (1 Cor 13.8). Perhaps, though, our ongoing mediation of God's glory to each other will continue—not of necessity, but in a mode of celebration. May we delight, both now and then, to chant about *the many-colored wisdom of*

---

[5]Crashaw, "Hymn to the Name of Jesus." The original poem uses the spelling "Pitty," which I have altered for clarity.

*God . . . according to the ages-old purpose . . . accomplished in Christ Jesus our Lord* (Eph 3.7–11), as we grow more and more into His likeness.

We have approached human mediation not as a redemptive category, but as a major trait of Christ's Church: we cannot be the Church without it. Mediation, in all its expressions (intercession, petition, teaching, sacraments, iconic representation, and even relics) leads us today to affirm both the discomfort of hierarchy and the comfort of mutuality. Our concern for each other is enlivened by the inexhaustible Spirit of God, and will never rob Jesus of His unique place, nor must it wane as the Christian family grows, as though we only had so much energy. We have it on good authority that our prayers come from the divine Source of *living water* that springs up eternally (Jn 4.14), that the Holy Spirit *groans* alongside us when we do not know how to pray (Rom 8.26–27), and that we are surrounded by a host of witnesses rather than simply interceding on our own (Heb 12.1). Indeed, we are assured that God has given us everything that we need pertaining to life and godliness (2 Pet 1.3). What may seem a meager widow's cruse will never run dry, for we are caught up in God's very own life as we help each other, and receive aid. Our mutual participation in this life of mediation is a deep secret at the center of our conjoined lives, binding us together with each other, as well as with the angelic hosts and the rest of God's creation.

St Paul recognized this wonder of the Church's mutuality when he described how the apostles held within them *a treasure in earthen vessels* (2 Cor 4.7), so that the focus would be not on them but on God's surpassing glory. In the same way, all of this is included in God's plan for the building up of His Body, the Church: the grace of the saints, including the Theotokos, who intercede for us; our tender prayers for those who have passed from our midst; our mutual and ordered prayers among those with whom we presently live; and our willingness to become "weak" for the strength of others. Only the mediation of the God-Man redeems, but all the little mediations, echoing His unspeakable gift, are gathered up in God's plan for our full salvation—both personally, and together. There is, in mediation, an expansiveness that corresponds to the utter generosity of God, which faces towards others, inviting them to join us. With Paul, then, *we also speak, knowing that the One who raised the Lord Jesus will raise us also with Jesus and bring us . . . into His presence . . . so that as grace extends to more and more people, it may increase thanksgiving, to the glory of God* (2 Cor 4.13–15).

# Abbreviations

ACC   Ancient Christian Commentary on Scripture. Eds. T. C. Oden *et al.* Downer's Grove, IL, Intervarsity Press, 1998–.

ANCL  Ante-Nicene Christian Library: Translations of the Writings of the Fathers down to AD 325. Edited by A. Donaldson and P. Roberts. Edinburgh: T & T Clark, 1867–97.

ANF   Ante-Nicene Fathers. Edited by A. Roberts and J. Donaldson. 10 volumes. Buffalo NY: Christian Literature, 1885–1896. Reprint, Peabody, MA: Hendrickson, 1994.

CCL   Corpus Christianorum. Series Latina. Turnhout, Belgium: Brepols, 1953–.

FC    Fathers of the Church: A New Translation. Edited by R. J. Deferrari, et al. Washington, DC: Catholic University of America Press, 1947–.

LCC   The Library of Christian Classics. 26 volumes. Edited by J. Baillie, et al. Philadelphia: Westminster Press, 1953–1966.

NPNF A Select Library of the Nicene and Post-Nicene Fathers of the Christian Church. Two series, 14 volumes each. Edited by P. Schaff, et al. Buffalo, NY: Christian Literature, 1887–1894; Reprint, Peabody, MA: Hendrickson, 1994.

PG    Patrologia cursus completus. Series Graeca. 166 volumes. Edited by J.-P. Migne. Paris: Migne, 1857–1886.

PL    Patrologiae cursus completus. Series Latina 221 volumes. Edited by J.-P. Migne. Paris: Migne, 1844–64.

# Bibliography

*1 Clement.* In *Apostolic Fathers.* Translated by J. B. Lightfoot. Edited by J. R. Harmer. London: Macmillan & Co., 1907. Pages 5–40 and 57–85.

*1 Enoch.* In *Old Testament Pseudepigrapha I.* Translated by E Isaac. Edited by James H. Charlesworth. New York: Doubleday, 1983. Pages 5–90.

*The Anaphora of The Holy Apostles Addai and Mari.* Translated by William Macomber as "The Ancient Form of the *Anaphora of the Apostles.*" In *East of Byzantium: Syria and Armenia in the Formative Period.* Edited by Nina Garsoïan, Thomas Mathews, and Robert Thomson. Washington, DC: Cumbarton Oaks Centre for Byzantine Studies, 1982. Pages 73–88.

Ambrose. *Of the Christian Faith.* NPNF² 10:201–314.

———. *Letters* 27. FC 26:140.

Auden, W. H. "As I Walked Out One Evening." In *Collected Poems.* New York: Vintage, 1991. Page 133.

Augustine. *The City of God.* In FC 14 and NPNF¹ 2:1–511.

———. *The Confessions, Revised: Saint Augustine,* volume 1. Translated by Maria Boulding. New York: New City Press, 2008.

————. *De Doctrina*. In NPNF[1] 2:519–97.

————. *Letter 149*. In FC 20:239–66.

————. *Sermon 77*. PL 38:483–90. English translation: *Sermon 27*. NPNF[1] 6:342–47.

————. *Tractates on John*. FC 14.

Botha, P. J. J. "The Gospel of Matthew and Women." *In die Skriflig* 37.3 (2003): 505–32.

Bultmann, Rudolph. *The New Testament and Mythology and Other Basic Writings*. Translated and edited by Schubert M. Ogden. Philadelphia, PA: Fortress, 1984.

Cassian, John. *On the Holy Fathers of Sketis and On Discrimination*. In *The Philokalia, The Complete Text*, Volume 1. Translated and edited by G. E. H. Palmer, Philip Sherrard, and Kallistos Ware. London: Faber and Faber, 1979. Pages 94–108.

Charles, Ronald. "Rahab: A Righteous Whore in James." *Neotestamentica* 45.2 (January 2011): 201–20.

Chromatius. *Tractate on Matthew 59*. In Corpus Christianorum. Series Latina, Volume 9. Turnhout, Belgium: Brepols, 1953.

Chrysologus, Peter. *Sermon 132*. CCL 24 and FC 17.

Chrysostom, John. *Commentary on Galatians*. PG 61. English translation: NPNF[1] 13:1–48.

————. *Homilies on the Gospel of John*. NPNF[1] 14.

————. *Homilies on the Gospel of Matthew*. PG 58:784. NPNF[1] 10.

————. *Homilies on 1 Timothy*. NPNF[1] 13:407–473.

————. *In Ascensionem*. PG 50:444–46.

Clement of Alexandria. *Miscellanies (Stromata)*. ANF 2:299–567.

Clément, Olivier. *You are Peter: An Orthodox Theologian's Reflection on the Exercise of Primal Papacy.* New York: New City Press, 2003 [1st French edition 1997].

Climacus, John. *The Ladder of Divine Ascent,* revised edition. Translated by Archimandrite Lazarus Moore. Brookline, MA: Holy Transfiguration Monastery, 2019 [1st ed. 1959].

Crashaw, Richard. "In the Holy Nativity of Our Lord" and "Hymn to the Name of Jesus." In *The Religious poems of Richard Crashaw.* Edited by R. A. Eric Shepherd. St Louis, MO: B Herder, 1914. Pages 30–42.

Cyprian, *Epistle 56.* ANCL 5:351–52.

Cyril of Alexandria. Fragment 215 in *Matthäus-Kommentare aus der griechischen Kirche* 224. Edited by Joseph Reuss. Berlin: Akademie-Verlag, 1957.

Dorotheos of Gaza. *Discourses and Sayings.* Translated by Eric P. Wheeler. Kalamazoo, MI: Cistercian Publications, 2008.

Evdokimov, Paul. *Woman and the Salvation of the World: A Christian Anthropology on the Charisms of Women.* Crestwood, NY: St Vladimir's Seminary Press, 1994 [1st French edition, 1983].

France, R. T. *The Gospel of Matthew.* Grand Rapids, MI: Eerdmans, 2007.

Frye, Northrop. *Anatomy of Criticism: Four Essays.* Princeton, NJ: Princeton University Press, 1957.

Gregory of Nazianzus. *On God and Christ: The Five Theological Orations and Two Letters to Cledonius.* Translated by Frederick Williams and Lionel Wickham. Popular Patristics Series 23. Crestwood, NY: St Vladimir's Seminary Press, 2002.

Gregory of Nyssa. *Against Eunomius.* NPNF$^2$ 5:33–314.

Hagner, Donald A. "Holiness and Ecclesiology: The Church in Matthew." In *Holiness and Ecclesiology in the New Testament*. Edited by Kent E. Brower and Andy Johnson. Grand Rapids, MI: Eerdmans, 2007. Pages 40–56.

Hauerwas, Stanley. *Brazos Theological Commentary on Matthew*. Grand Rapids, MI: Brazos, 2015 [1st edition, 2006].

Humphrey, Edith M. *Further Up and Further In: Orthodox Conversations with C. S. Lewis on Scripture and Tradition*. Yonkers, NY: St Vladimir's Seminary Press, 2017.

————. *Scripture and Tradition: What the Bible Really Says*. Grand Rapids, MI: Baker Academic, 2013.

————. *Grand Entrance: Worship on Earth as in Heaven*. Grand Rapids, MI: Brazos, 2011.

————. *Ecstasy and Intimacy: When the Holy Spirit Meets the Human Spirit*. Grand Rapids, MI: Eerdmans, 2005.

————. *Joseph and Aseneth*. Guide to Apocrypha and Pseudepigrapha 8. Sheffield: Sheffield Academic Press, 2000.

Isaac of Nineveh. *Ascetical Homilies*. In *On Ascetical Life*. Translated by Mary Hansbury. Popular Patristics Series 11. Crestwood, NY: St Vladimir's Seminary Press, 1989.

John of Damascus. *Three Treatises on the Divine Images*. Translated by Andrew Louth. Popular Patristics Series 24. Crestwood, NY: St Vladimir's Seminary Press, 2003.

Kadari, Tamar. "Rahab: Midrash and Aggadah." *Shalvi/Hyman Encyclopedia of Jewish Women*. Jewish Women's Archive. (Viewed on April 13, 2022). <https://jwa.org/encyclopedia/article/rahab-midrash-and-aggadah>, December 31, 1999.

Lewis, C. S. *The Abolition of Man: Or, Reflections on Education with Special Reference to the Teaching of English in the Upper Forms of Schools*. New York: HarperOne, 2001 [1st edition, 1944].

———. An *Experiment in Criticism*. Cambridge University Press, 1988 [1st edition, 1961].

———. *The Collected Letters of C. S. Lewis*, three volumes. Edited by Walter Hooper. HarperSanFrancisco, 2004–2007.

———. *Letters To Malcolm: Chiefly on Prayer*. London: Collins / Fontana, 1966 [1st edition, 1964].

———. *Mere Christianity*. New York: HarperCollins Paperback, 2001 [1st edition, 1952].

———. *Miracles: A Preliminary Study*. New York: HarperOne, 1974 [1st edition, 1947].

———. *Till We Have Faces: A Myth Retold*. Grand Rapids, MI: Eerdmans, 1966 [1st edition, 1956].

*Lexham English Septuagint*. Bellingham, WA: Lexham Press, 2019.

Lossky, Vladimir. *Mystical Theology of the Eastern Church*. London: James Clarke and Co., 1957 [1st French ed. 1944].

*Martyrdom of Polycarp*. In *The Apostolic Fathers*, volume 2. Translated by Kirsopp Lake. Loeb Classical Library 25. Cambridge, MA: Harvard University Press, 1950 [1st edition, 1913]. Pages 312–45.

Origen. *Commentaria in Evangelium secundum Matthaeum*. PG 13:829–1800.

Meyendorff, John. *The Primacy of Peter: Essays in Ecclesiology and the Early Church*. Crestwood, NY: St Vladimir's Press, 1992.

Schmemann, Alexander. *For the Life of the World: Sacraments and Orthodoxy,* 3rd edition. Yonkers, NY: St Vladimir's Seminary Press, 2018.

Selvidge, M. J. "Violence, Woman, and the Future of the Matthean Community: A Redactional Critical Study." *Union Seminary Quarterly Review* 39 (1984): 213–23.

*Shepherd of Hermas.* In *The Apostolic Fathers,* volume 2. Translated by Kirsopp Lake. Loeb Classical Library 25. Cambridge, MA: Harvard University Press, 1950 [1st edition, 1913]. Pages 1–305.

Stăniloae, Dumitru. *The Experience of God: Orthodox Dogmatic Theology, Volume 6: The Fulfillment of Creation.* Translated and edited by Ioan Ioniță. Brookline, MA: Holy Cross Orthodox Press, 2013.

Talbert, Charles H. *Matthew.* Paidea Commentary Series. Grand Rapids, MI: Eerdmans, 2010.

Tertullian. *On the Flesh of Christ.* ANF 3:521–42.

———. *De Oratione* [*On Prayer*]. In *Tertullian: Disciplinary, Moral, and Ascetical Works.* Translated by Rudolph Arbesmann, Emily Joseph Daly, and Edwin A. Quain. Fathers of the Church 40. Washington, DC: The Catholic University of America Press, 1962. Pages 157–88.

Theodore of Mopsuestia. *Commentary on 1 Timothy. In Epistolas b. Pauli commentarii.* 2 vols. Edited by H. B. Swete. Cambridge University Press, 1880–1882.

Zirpolo, Lilian H. *Historical Dictionary of Baroque Art and Architecture.* Washington, DC: Rowan and Littlefield, 2018.

# Index of Scripture and Other Ancient Sources

# Index of Subjects and Names

Samaritan woman. *See* Photini
Satan, 44, 61, 91
Schmemann, Alexander, 110
Scriptures, x, 2–3, 6, 8, 12–13, 20, 22,
    31–32, 36, 43, 47, 52–54, 66, 68,
    77, 84, 85, 92, 98, 99, 111, 118,
    119, 123, 146, 161. *See also* Bible.
Second Coming, 26
Selvidge, J. J., 138
seraphim. *See* angels
Sermon of the Mount, 42
shepherd, 29
Simon Magus, 55–59, 121
simony, 56
sin, 1, 9, 19, 21–22, 56, 59, 80–82,
    85–86, 102, 150–151, 157
Sinai, 25
Solomon, 51, 114, 133, 152, 155
spirit, human, 120, 163
Stăniloae, Dumitru, 26, 27
Stephen, 13
Symeon, the Prophet, 145
*synaxis*, 50, 55

Talbert, Charles H., 133–134, 136
teacher, 24, 78, 80, 111
temple, 59–60, 68, 115, 145, 151–157, 160
Tertullian, 18, 162
testimony, 52, 120
thanksgiving, 7, 14, 75, 108, 152, 169.
    *See also* prayer and Eucharist
Theodore of Mopsuestia, 18
Theodoret of Cyrus, 20
*theōsis*, 27, 36, 53
Theotokos. *See* Mary, the Virgin
Thomas, Apostle, 32, 90, 147
Throne of God, 23, 26, 87, 97–98, 104,
    151–152, 154, 156–158
time, 47
Torah, 2, 29, 49, 53
Transfiguration, 51, 88–89, 102

Trinity, Holy, 2, 5, 15, 25, 26, 28, 41,
    48, 89–90 144, 156, 161

Valentinus, 18
Van Deusen, Mary, 72
vine, 29–30, 149
vision
    of Abercius, 74
    of apostolic council, 63
    of disciples, 88
    of Ezekiel, 157
    of Gregory of Nyssa, 26
    of Isaiah, 144–145, 156–157
    of Jacob, 93
    of John, 6, 77, 86–87, 97–98, 113,
        152
    of Maximos the Confessor, 26
    of Peter, 62
    of Zechariah, 94
water, 31, 32, 57–58, 66, 105, 108–110,
    114, 121, 154–155, 168. *See also*
    baptism
Wesley, Charles, 23, 146
wine, 55, 66, 108, 109, 110, 114, 121. *See
    also* Eucharist
witness, 5, 29, 31, 36, 52–55, 61, 72,
    74, 77, 80, 86, 89–92, 101–102,
    113, 123–124, 139, 146, 148, 166,
    168. *See also* martyrdom and
    testimony
women, 5, 47, 51, 58, 102, 126–129,
    132–134, 138, 139, 140, 141, 145,
    149, 150, 152, 155, 159
Word. *See* Logos
worship, 50–51, 54, 86, 87, 94, 95,
    97–98, 99, 103, 104, 105, 107,
    108, 110, 113–118, 121, 122, 134,
    135, 140, 144, 148, 149, 155–160.
    *See also* Liturgy
YHWH, i, 15, 29
Zion, 152